Ralf Coykendall's

DUCK DECOYS
AND HOW TO
RIG THEM

Ralf Coykendall's

DUCK DECOYS
AND HOW TO
RIG THEM

Revised by Ralf Coykendall, Jr.

Introduction by Gene Hill

Decorative drawings by Bob Cary

The Lyons Press

Printed in the United States of America

10   9   8   7   6

**Library of Congress
Cataloging-in-Publication Data**

Coykendall, Ralf.
  [Duck decoys and how to rig them]
Ralf Coykendall's duck decoys and how to rig
them/revised by Ralf Coykendall, Jr.:
introduction by Gene Hill: decorative drawings
by Bob Cary. p.   cm.   Reprint. Originally
published: Piscataway, N.J.: Winchester Press,
©1983. ISBN 1-55821-039-3: $12.95
1. Decoys (Hunting) I. Coykendall, Ralf W.
(Ralf Wales), 1929–   . II. Title. III. Title: Duck
decoys and how to rig them.
SK335.C60   1989   799.2'4841—dc20
89-12682   CIP

DEDICATION

In my handsomely bound copy of the first edition of this fine book, my father wrote: *to my favorite gunning companion.* He would approve of my dedicating this edition of his book to his grandson and namesake, my favorite gunning companion, Ralf Coykendall III.

RCjr

RALF COYKENDALL   1892–1968

Contents

Introduction

One of the reasons I'm writing an introduction to this delightful book on duck hunting is that Ralf Coykendall, Jr. threatened not to give me a superb miniature carving he'd done of a nesting woodcock, which I suddenly discovered I could not live without.

Another reason is that I'm glad to see that Ralf, Sr. was right when he predicted that waterfowl gunning would get harder as the pressure increased and that it ought to turn shooters into hunters. Just going out with a guide or a buddy and messing around is not the worst way to spend a day, but far better is the pleasure of knowing how to set a proper rig for the place, the weather, and the species.

If a lot of the thrill of the sport is the achievement of shooting skills (as it is to me) so, too, is the challenge of decoying your birds where you want them. There is a vast and important difference between shooting the occasional duck and calling yourself a duck hunter.

There isn't much sense in telling you that this little book is a treasure trove of information and is good reading as well; you can see that for yourself. I revere its attitude. I've read this book fairly often, and now I see that Ralf, in his own gentle way, was creating a set of rules by which a sportsman would play the game—getting him involved in the right traditions and vastly extending the pleasure of gunning beyond the simple pulling of the trigger.

One more, and final reason, is that Ralf's words were always important to me and I'm delighted that you're about to see why. As a way of introduction I thought you might enjoy the following, written not in sadness, but in a moment of wondering reflection very soon after Ralf was gone.

The Old Duck Hunter died the other day, 75 years old and suddenly he's gone like a black in full flight.

But the things he took with him! The stories that only he could tell—because only he remembered. The subtle inflection, the nicety of a turn of phrase, the eye lost to use for a minute while it turned backward ... 40 ... 50 ... 60 years. Everything was different then in the times gone long ago. I'm sure the hay smelled sweeter in the fall, the air was crisper, the ducks wilder, and the hand-polished Parkers threw better patterns with what they used to call "St. Louis 3's." The clothes were tougher, the whiskey smoother, the weather sharper, and they shot bigger and smarter birds and more of them.

God! How I miss it. I could listen with closed eyes and see the fieldstone fireplaces in the legendary, long-lost duck clubs blazing with the crack of pine knots that talked back while busily sludging smoke into the spitting promise of tomorrow's squall. Not many left who knew and drank and gunned and laughed with the likes of Shang Wheeler, Joel Barber, and Colonel Sheldon.

He was an old young man, whatever that means. Just a few days ago we had drinks together. Old Forester on the rocks with a touch of bitters for him and I think I had a martini. We didn't talk for the first few minutes, just stood at the bar and steeped in the pleasure of each other's company. We liked each other and words never seemed necessary at first or even appropriate. Then we began chatting about guns and duck loads. As usual he favored 4's and I favored 6's. He liked oversized decoys and I agreed. And we ordered lunch. He was a spare man, and tough.

But we kidded a lot. I teased him about his skeet shooting and he reminded me that trap shooters were often seen in the field without neckties. Lunch was over and he remarked that he wasn't feeling well and I never saw him again.

If a man can love another man I guess that I loved Ralf. I loved the things he stood for and the way he stood for them. I could tell you that I miss him but that wouldn't be saying very much. So I can't tell you anything, except that he's gone and things have changed. Duck blinds aren't exactly the same anymore and neither is bourbon whiskey. And that's a lot of change to me. A lot of change. And I'd rather not go into it more deeply, because you know what I mean. Because I can't.

I hope you have an Old Duck Hunter in your life and I hope he lives in your blind ... and shares your whiskey forever. Like Ralf, I'm sure, will do with me. I have a hollow space that only he can fill ... in moments that we all have between flights ... between life's little things ... between the distant promise in the call of geese and the sudden flare of setting wings ... between the point and the flush ... and in the darkening moments between the end of the day and the start of tomorrow.

Gene Hill

Foreword

It is probably more difficult, day in and day out, to shoot today's duck limit than it was to kill the legal boatload of a generation or so ago. The great flights are gone and so, too, are live decoys, baiting, and batteries. The unobservant duck hunter may report good shooting or bad, may complain of the low bag limit one week and of the scarcity of birds on his flyway the next. The shrewd wildfowler speaks of educated ducks and concentrates his attention on decoys.

Gun clubs whose locations, stands, and equipment have remained unchanged for fifty years are finding it desirable to replace their old decoys with more modern and far better new ones. I know a family of baymen who have gunned the same general area for three generations. Grandfather, son, and grandson have guided their "sports" in the same marsh for well over half a century. The type of boats and blinds they use has not varied, but the grandson has found it essential to replace the old rig with new and bigger decoys to entice ducks and geese within gun range for his customers.

Old decoys may be profitable items for an antique dealer, but they are not an asset in a gunner's rig. The best modern decoys well rigged are needed for present shooting conditions. The days are long gone when clods of heaped-up mud or tin cans painted black would bring the ducks in.

Some of the old-timers had wonderful decoys—they made them—but most of their decoys were only fair by today's standards. We can buy far better decoys than they had, but cannot match their knowledge of duck and geese and how to rig for them. These old-timers packed more shooting days into a single season than most of us can manage in a lifetime. Some of the things they did were dependent upon highly specialized knowledge or familiarity with local conditions. We cannot equal their experience, but we can learn some of the basic things they did and profit from them.

Few who gun now and none who learn to gun in the years ahead can have the pleasure of, or acquire the information that was to be gained by, shooting with and watching and listening to the old baymen, market hunters, and guides. They were wise men, extraordinary shots, and skilled naturalists. Many of them are gone. Most of those I have known were old men when I met them. Ren Overton was seventy-five and Captain Billy Rand past eighty when I first shot from their blinds. George Washington Snow was an escaped slave who brought his ideas on ducks and rigging up the Underground Railway from the Deep South to Lake Ontario. He must have been close to the century mark when my grandfather sent me out with him with my first single-barrel shotgun. Charles DoVille was making decoys, building his famous version of the St. Lawrence skiff, and guiding for my Grandfather Chase at the turn of the century.

These, and others, constituted a link to a different time. They bridged the gap between shooting as we know it and the almost legendary days of black powder, market gunning, spring shooting, and vast flights of birds. I have decided to set down some of their lore before the last of them picks up his rig some cold, windy night and rows off into the darkness—his season closed forever.

RALF COYKENDALL   1955

[xiv]

My father was a great believer in arranging and rearranging his decoys to meet a variety of ever-changing conditions. It has been said that he enjoyed this rigging and rerigging more than any other facet of gunning. He did. I am certain, therefore, that he would approve of my looking after his rig, touching up here and there and straightening a twisted line or two—not really changing anything, you understand. There is no need of change. This is my father's book as he wrote it. Dad has joined the old baymen, market hunters, and guides he wrote about, and picked up his rig for the last time. His book survives.

RALF COYKENDALL JR.   1983

THESE ARE

HENS   DRAKES

MALLARD

BLACK

PINTAIL

WIDGEON

BLUE-WINGED TEAL

CINNAMON TEAL

GREEN-WINGED TEAL

BLUE GOOSE   BRANT

THE DECOYS

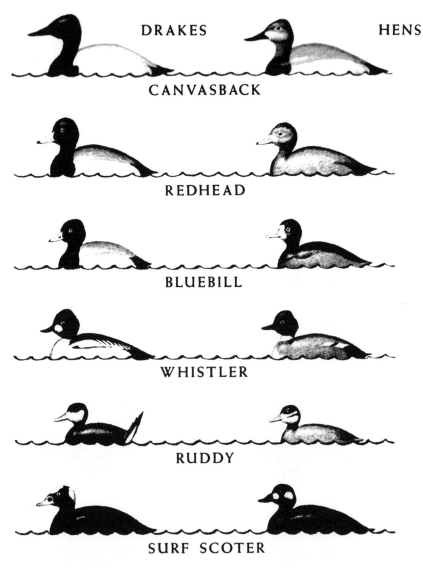

DRAKES   HENS

CANVASBACK

REDHEAD

BLUEBILL

WHISTLER

RUDDY

SURF SCOTER

Note: In Black Duck, Brant, and Geese, sexes are alike in plumage.

SNOW GOOSE   CANADA GOOSE

1.

Terminology

When duck hunters from different parts of the country meet it sometimes takes a little while for them to understand each other's terms. When the hunters are of different generations the variation in names is even more marked. A new gunner might have to dig into his books to be sure just what the now-illegal battery looked like or to learn why it was considered so deadly.

The phrases I employ are bound to be colored by my environment and my associates through the years I have gunned. Captain Billy Rand referred to his rig of decoys as a *stool* and Charles DoVille called his a *spread*. I have tried to use the most generally accepted terminology, but such colloquialisms are a part of the language of duck hunting. No one misunderstands these expressions for long.

An illustration of geographically different nomenclature is in the names used for scaup. On the East coast they are called *broadbill*, and inland on fresh water they are called *bluebill*. If the question comes up, gunners from either area will quickly explain that they distinguish between them by designating the greater scaup broadbill and the lesser scaup bluebill. I am not suggesting that they do not separate these birds in their thinking, nor that they fail to recognize the differences in size

[3]

and plumage. They do, of course, but you will have to keep a sharp ear tuned to hear either of the scaup called anything but broadbill on salt water or bluebill on fresh water.

Decoys, too, have many names. The words *stool* and *decoy* are synonymous. A generation ago older guides referred to their decoys as *blocks*. *Stool* is frequently used in a plural or collective sense and then it is interchangeable with *set, rig, spread, layout, pattern,* and so on. Ducks either stool to your decoys or decoy to your stool (or stools).

The word *stool* is an obvious contraction from *stool duck* or *stool goose*. In many areas live decoys, especially geese, were tethered to a stool which consisted of a flat board nailed to the top of a pointed pole. The point of the pole was thrust into the sand or mud bottom so its platform was about two inches under water. The duck or goose could swim about in a confined circle or climb onto the platform to preen or sleep.

Ducks and geese are said to *trade* or *use* in areas where they are accustomed to feed or move regularly. When they gather in large groups, particularly on open water, they are *rafted* or *rafted up*.

Decoy, probably of Dutch origin, is an ancient word. It appears first in its present form in English reports of wildfowling in the early seventeenth century. Decoys antedate their name. Like many basic inventions, they appear to have been separately developed on several continents thousands of years ago. There is reference to lures for wildfowl in accounts of prehistoric Mesopotamia. The American Indian was shooting canvasback over decoys made of dyed straw and feathers hundreds of years before Leif Ericson or Columbus stepped on these shores. When we set out a rig of decoys we are engaged in an ancient routine.

2.

Basic Types of Decoys

Ducks are divided into two basic groups—the diving ducks and the shoal-water ducks. Decoys, like the ducks they are to lure, should have the same characteristics distinguishable at any distance. The diving ducks are high forward and low aft, and the shoal-water ducks are low forward and high aft.

Within these two basic groups are the individual species varying in size, shape, and plumage painting, the hens being unlike the drakes, except for a few species like the black ducks. If a duck hunter wished to have a set of decoys for every kind of duck and goose hunted somewhere in the United States or Canada, he would need about four hundred decoys. This would give him a reasonable number of each, but far less of some species than many qualified gunners consider sufficient for a rig.

In the late twenties, when batteries were still legal, I shot on Great South Bay with Red Harris, a famous guide in that Long Island area, who used two hundred and fifty broadbill decoys in a single rig. Thoroughly competent guides rig one hundred to one hundred and fifty broadbill for shooting among the rocky islands off Sachem's Head, Connecticut. They rig in deep, cold, rough water and it is a laborious job to set out and pick up from their small dories. They never rig a single decoy they think unnecessary.

Rigs of over a hundred canvasback and redhead are not unusual for sneak-boat shooting near Detroit on Lake St. Clair, the Detroit River, and Lake Erie. Very large rigs of decoys are still used on the Susquehanna Flats of Chesapeake Bay.

A large rig does not ensure success, however, and in some cases is unnecessary and may be wrong. The factors controlling a suitable number of decoys vary. They include area of water, location, competition, type of blind or boat, and the variety of ducks to be hunted. A friend who year in and year out gets excellent shooting and almost always kills his limit has a total rig of only fifty-four decoys. He rarely, if ever, uses them all at one time. He has a dozen blacks, half a dozen each of mallard, pintail, and Canada geese, and two dozen bluebill. His decoys are the finest he can buy, he is an expert at rigging, a deadly shot, and the marsh and lake where he shoots provide exceptional conditions. The point is that he has worked out a rig that fits his needs. Most duck hunters will find that to assemble a good set of decoys takes time. It is not just a matter of going out and buying them. Local conditions must be studied and even seasoned duck hunters will find it essential to do some experimenting when in a new location, adding some decoys and discarding others before they have a rig that serves their particular requirements. A good rig is never static. Each season is likely to produce some situation that calls for changes and improvements. For example, a mallard decoy was unusual in a western New England rig ten years ago. We rarely saw mallards. Now we kill almost as many mallards as we do black ducks and the wise gunners are adding mallard decoys to their rigs.

For various reasons decoys are not made to duplicate all species. Many duck will stool to decoys of some other kind. Wood duck will stool to mallards and ringneck decoy readily to bluebill. No distinction is made between the lesser and the greater scaup—one set of decoys serves for both.

The food value of some ducks does not justify trying to decoy them, but there are local exceptions. The flavor of a duck

[8]

depends on its diet, and certain ducks not considered worth the expenditure of ammunition in some parts of the country are thought of as table delicacies elsewhere.

Few duck hunters will need decoys of all species since the various ducks and geese are not common to all flyways. The East-coast gunner, for instance, has no need of decoys for blue geese or cinnamon teal, and the inland shooter needs no brant decoys.

The following table lists the decoys generally in use and customarily available to the duck hunter. The quantities of each species indicated are merely suggestions of what many would consider an average rig.

TABLE OF DECOYS

SHOAL WATER DUCKS

Species	Hens	Drakes	Total
Mallard	6	6	12
Pintail	6	6	12
Widgeon	6	6	12
Bluewing Teal	6	6	12
Cinnamon Teal	6	6	12
Greenwing Teal	6	6	12
Black Duck	Plumage of sexes alike		12
Blue Goose	Plumage of sexes alike		12
Canada Goose	Plumage of sexes alike		12
Snow Goose	Plumage of sexes alike		12

DIVING DUCKS

Species	Hens	Drakes	Total
Bluebill (Scaup)	30	30	60
Canvasback	30	30	60
Redhead	30	30	60
Ruddy	12	12	24
White-winged Scoter	24	24	48
Whistler (Golden Eye)	30	30	60

3.

What Is a Good Decoy?

Decoy shows and decoy-makers' contests have contributed a great deal to the improvement of the design and qualities of decoys in recent years. So far as I can learn, the first decoy show was an informal affair held at Bellport, Long Island, in the summer of 1923, and they have been held intermittently ever since. A folder describing the conditions under which the most recent National Show was held said in part: "Such shows give makers and users of decoys an opportunity to exchange ideas and designs, and to advance the art and craft of decoy making."

Relatively few of the millions of duck hunters have seen these shows, but gunners everywhere owe a debt of gratitude to those responsible for them. As a result of the shows the "breed" of decoys has constantly improved. Excellent factory-made decoys are available to the gunner today, at reasonable prices, which make the "good" decoys of a few years ago seem rather crude affairs.

Having served for a number of years on the committees that wrote the rules and organized the judging of decoys at the National Sportsman's Shows in New York, I have had an opportunity to hear some very expert opinion on the subject of decoys. Joel Barber, Charles E. Wheeler, Lynn Bogue Hunt, Thomas M. Marshall, Eugene V. Connett, William Mackey—to

[11]

name only a few of those who have judged the decoys—spent hours comparing and discussing them. The knowledge and experience of these men covered almost every variety of duck hunting in this country and in much of Canada and Mexico. Several of them are decoy collectors and two have written books about decoys. Their composite opinion, I think, can be summed up by saying *a good decoy is one which under a given set of circumstances best serves the gunner.* They realized that decoys designed for offshore work in rough water where sea-keeping ability and great visibility are important factors will be ideal for one man, but far from ideal for another shooting on an inland pond to which he must carry his decoys through a mile of brush or swamp. He wants lightweight and compact decoys. While recognizing the merits of special decoys for special purposes, the only decoys seriously considered for prizes by the judges at these National Shows were those best suited to serve most gunners under average rather than special conditions.

Except for lightweight decoys or silhouette "stick-ups" for use on land, the first quality required in a decoy is that it act like a good boat. It must lie well at anchor. It ought to be steady and not skid across the waves, dip or roll excessively, or be blown sideways by every little gust of wind. The paint ought to be flat and dull to avoid reflecting light. Most hunters have observed that ducks are likely to move immediately after a rain. However, they will not decoy properly if the sun comes out or if the sky is particularly light until the decoys have dried off and no longer shine.

Now and then someone turns up with the prodigious idea of removing the skin and feathers from a duck and using them to cover a shaped block. It sounds wonderful to those without experience, but it never works. Instead of looking like a duck, these creations appear tiny and bedraggled.

Duck hunters sometimes use floats or stick-ups to make the birds they have killed serve as additional decoys. In a few hours they lose their fresh and lifelike quality and begin to look like what they are—dead ducks. This is an expedient to be used only if you are extremely short of decoys. I have never seen qualified guides resort to this device.

Good decoys are not exact copies of ducks. There is something of a "cartoon" about them in that their size, shape, or painting are sometimes exaggerated. The most frequently exaggerated quality is size, and if the duck hunter questions the effectiveness of oversize decoys let him try the following experiment. Use normal and oversize decoys in the same rig and keep them separate in such a way that no advantage of position benefits either group. All else being equal, ducks will stool to the oversize decoys ninety per cent of the time. How much oversize is a question frequently asked. I have seen mallard and black duck decoys bigger than live geese and Canada goose decoys literally as big as sugar barrels—all used successfully. Except when I need very lightweight decoys, the rig I shoot over is made up of decoys about fifty per cent oversize.

It is possible, but not particularly effective, to use oversize with normal or standard decoys. It is definitely wrong to mix good and bad decoys. An experience shared with an old-time guide and friend last year taught us both this lesson. He had changed his rig, replacing his outmoded old blocks with new decoys. In his boat while running out to the blind he told me he planned to rig some pintail. He explained that until the last few days there had been no pintail shooting in that bay for several years. "Didn't figure any reason for buying new pintail decoys," he said. "Pintail suddenly came back, so we'll have to use old ones if we use any. Guess they'll work."

Along with his new mallard, widgeon, and goose decoys he set a dozen old pintails. There was only a light breeze, hardly more than a ripple on the water, but even so the old round-bottomed decoys rolled. Several bunches of mallards looked us over, but none came in. After a couple of hours in which we had

[13]

no shooting the guide said, "You know what? I think them damn' pintail blocks a-rockin' and a-shinin' is our trouble. I'm goin' to take 'em up."

He did and the next birds came in. The behavior of the old decoys was in direct contrast to the steady riding of the new, big, flat-bottomed decoys and this no doubt made him conscious of the shortcomings of the pintail blocks. A different day with heavier weather which would have kept all the decoys in motion might have kept him from spotting the imperfections in the old decoys. Fortunately he did spot our trouble.

Unless the duck hunter expects to shoot invariably on calm, protected water, small inland ponds or lakes, he had best buy decoys that are oversize. They should have flat bottoms and be almost half as wide as they are long. They should have keels and ballast to make them ride well, and to behave properly on the water they should weigh about as much as the duck they represent. Some gunners consider self-righting an important attribute in a decoy. This is especially true for diving-duck decoys because they are frequently rigged by throwing both decoy and anchor overboard at the same time and if decoys are used that do not right themselves, much time is wasted turning them right side up.

Decoys should have great stability so that in heavy seas there is no danger of their rolling over and floating bottom up.

Naturally contented ducks lie with their heads down or turned as they preen or sleep or else they are feeding. When alerted they lie with heads erect and all pointed upwind, as though likely to take off. Be adroit, therefore, and buy some of your decoys with adjustable heads and set the heads in a variety of positions so your rig has that "contented" look.

Decoys are worth what you pay for them. Well-made decoys should last a lifetime and it is an economy to buy the best you can find. I would far rather shoot over a few good decoys than over twice as many indifferent stool. You do not have to buy an entire rig all at one time. Start with a few good decoys and buy more when you can.

4.

Decoys for Special Conditions

One of my choice possessions is a lightweight folding decoy given to me by Rocco DiMarco of Detroit. It was made and used by his father. It had to be light and compact, for he rode to his shooting on a bicycle and carried his decoys in a basket strapped to the handle bars. This most ingenious decoy folds flat when the anchor line is wound around it. When the anchor line is unwound a wire keel with a lead weight drops down, the hinged profile snaps up and is held erect by a silver wire spring, which Mr. DiMarco drew and forged to the proper temper. The unusual anchor is a lead triangle with a distinguishing D cast in the mold. This is a true example of a decoy planned to fit the special needs of a purposeful duck hunter.

Another example of an original effort to create compact decoys is the "Sodus Bay" decoy. These particular two-piece silhouettes when taken apart were stored under the decks of a one-man layout boat. Although the boat was small, a hundred of these bluebill decoys could be stored aboard. When on the shooting ground the profiles of the ducks were slid into their bases and locked there by galvanized hooks. When anchored they made an impressive spread and the owner stretched out in his tiny "punkin seed" had excellent shooting.

A rig that always amused me was developed by a partridge-shooting neighbor. Soon after we started our usual swing up into the hills for ruffed grouse, we passed a pothole which sometimes held a few ducks. We always sneaked up prepared to jump them if they were "in" when we got there. One year when he found no ducks on the pond he took three black bladders from toy footballs out of his pocket, blew them up, and tied their rubber-valve stems with a long piece of cord which he also used as an anchor line by tying a stone to the other end. "Figure some lonesome ducks might see 'em," he said. "They might stick around till we get back down here this afternoon."

Such simple strategy sometimes pays off.

LINCOLN SLAT GOOSE AND REGULAR GOOSE DECOY

FIGURE 1

Joseph Lincoln of Accord, Massachusetts, famous as a decoy-maker, perfected a vastly oversize goose stool consisting of a slat frame covered with painted canvas. These were very large, but I have seen bigger and far cruder goose decoys made by covering sugar barrels with canvas and hastily painting them in a gray, black, and white pattern to resemble a goose.

Lincoln's shop was an aromatic place to visit, full of the odors of fresh pine, tarred rope, and the oils and turpentines of his paints. The floor was covered with the packed shavings from thousands of decoys. It was easier, he said, to raise his work bench by splicing onto the legs now and then than it would be to sweep the shavings out and burn them.

Fortunately, most duck hunters can find whatever they need in lightweight or extra-large decoys among those already on the market. For the gunner who shoots on protected water but must tote his decoys through swamps, brush, or mud for long distances, several lightweight types are available. Plastic decoys, when used without keels, are light enough so a man can carry a dozen in a pack on his back. For the goose hunter there are several kinds of folding silhouette decoys on the market for use as stick-ups.

The gunner who shoots on open water may want oversize decoys and they can be bought from a variety of sources. Size makes for great visibility, of course, but not all big decoys are necessarily seaworthy. I have shot over some handmade, oversize bluebill decoys that made a great show but had to be taken in because they rolled over when a sea built up. They were replaced by some old decoys, far too small, but they did float right side up in the heavy seas.

Years ago we were shooting on Shinnecock Bay, Long Island, in a terrific blow. We had killed our limits early, picked up, and were back at camp sitting, as Charlie Bussanih, our guide, said, "in the shelter of a fire and a little whisky," congratulating ourselves on our bag and on being in out of the storm. We had had trouble all day with some of the decoys flipping over and this led to us talking about the seaworthiness of decoys—big and little. Charlie made the point that decoys were like boats, and size had practically nothing to do with seaworthiness. He cited the whaleboats used by the Coast Guard, which put to sea in any weather, even when big ships were in trouble.

Knowing that he had served in the Coast Guard, I asked him how much sea he thought one of their whaleboats could stand. He said that he did not know, but the regulations called for boat drill, which meant launching the boat through the surf, every day except when too rough. He had been transferred while in the service to the Montauk Point Station, and finding that they had boat drill every day, he asked one of the old hands what the skipper considered *too rough.* "Don't know," was the reply; "bin here seven years an' it ain't bin too rough yit."

[19]

5.

Goose and Brant Decoys

There are fourteen or fifteen varieties of geese and brant, but not all are shot and only four types of decoys are used for them—except under rare conditions. Brant are coastal birds and shooting them has been under close restriction; there is only a limited and a regional interest in brant decoys, and as a result they are hard to find. Several manufacturers will make them on special order if given enough time. Since the black brant of the Pacific and the American brant of the Atlantic are similar, one type of decoy will serve on either coast.

"Commonest, best known and most widely distributed and most desired of all geese is the Canada," says Dr. William Bruette in his fine book, *American Duck, Goose and Brant Shooting*. In corn fields, on sand bars, in salt marshes, and along the great river flyways Canada geese are hunted, and decoys in one form or another are available almost anywhere. Decoys for blue geese and snow geese are not so common but can be obtained, as can brant decoys.

Silhouette decoys are frequently used for geese, especially in Midwestern grain fields and on sand bars along the Mississippi River. The best of these are so made that when they are set up they expand into a sort of triangular-shaped body that, viewed from overhead, gives a semblance of solidity. When using the

[21]

old, thin silhouettes it is important to set them facing in all directions so that some of them will be visible to geese from wherever they approach. Many geese are killed over silhouette decoys and they are not to be overlooked if you shoot on land and if their lack of weight is important to you.

Whenever conditions allow, I much prefer full-bodied decoys although they are heavier to handle. Floating decoys are necessarily full-bodied and are made from plastic, balsa, cork, pine, or cedar. While these decoys are costly, you do not need many and with proper care they will last indefinitely. Oversize goose decoys are recommended, especially if you shoot in competition with other goose rigs.

In some regions experienced gunners use enormous oversize decoys as *tollers*. Several of these are set some distance outside the goose rig—the theory being that they will be seen from immense distances and birds will swing toward them. By the time geese are near enough to suspect these giants they see the regular goose rig and will head for it. This practice is fairly common on Cape Cod where goose shooting has always been a specialty. In the days of live decoys, geese were trained to fly up when released from their pens, trying to lead passing flocks into range over the decoys.

Canada geese are wary birds and the best decoys are needed. It is wise, if you can, to buy goose decoys with adjustable heads or with heads set in different positions such as sleepers, preeners, and feeders. When shooting from a shore blind, place some of your goose decoys on the water and if possible have a few of them on shore. Geese are likely to be ashore part of the time.

A brant-shooting incident proves that decoys are not always hard to get and also illustrates a capable guide's resourcefulness. Several of us were shooting in eastern Shinnecock Bay with Charles Bussanih. He quickly identified a wavering line on the horizon as brant, although he had told me the day before that he had not seen brant on the bay for twenty years. This flock of about sixty brant passed near us without apparently giving our rig a glance, and lit on the bay half a mile away. During the day several other smaller flocks put in an appearance.

I asked Charlie about decoying them and he answered, "They're easy enough to kill when you get 'em in range, but hard to decoy. We ought to have some brant stool."

It was after seven o'clock that night when Charlie dropped us off at our hotel; it was four the next morning when he came to pick us up and drive us to his dock. "Look out for those decoys in the back of the boat," he warned us, "the paint on 'em ain't really dry."

I never learned what else he did in the seven or eight hours he was home; but he had made and painted a dozen brant decoys.

"It wasn't such a chore," he explained. "I'd been figurin' on makin' some oversize blacks and had some cork bodies glued up. Only had to shape 'em some. Had some goose heads sawed out that were a mite small. Just right for brant. Dowled some keels on and used ballast off some old redheads. Painted 'em and rigged some anchor lines. Wasn't such a job and they aren't too good. Ain't any eyes in 'em and the paint ain't dry."

We got some black paint on our hands helping Charlie rig that morning, but we killed a limit of brant.

6.

Good Decoys and Where to Buy Them

There are three sources from which the duck hunter may buy decoys. He can buy from local sporting-goods stores, order by mail, or find some local bayman or guide who will make decoys for him.

If you buy from a sporting-goods dealer, you have the advantage of seeing what you are buying, but you are limited by his stock. Providing the dealer has a large and varied assortment of normal and oversize decoys in different grades and prices, this is probably the best source. If he carries only a few decoys of a single grade and there is no real choice, you may do better buying by mail.

There are a number of reliable mail-order sources for decoys. Picking decoys from pictures and the glowing descriptions in catalogs can be hazardous. The safe plan is to order samples. Most mail-order suppliers have a special price for single decoys to enable prospective purchasers to order a few and look them over and try them out afloat.

Making decoys used to be a regular off-season activity for market hunters and guides, and at one time most of the fine decoys came from their work benches. There are very few of these craftsmen still to be found. Their workshops are fascinating places to visit and their decoys usually excellent. One thing to remember in dealing with them is that they may be specialists and make a fine decoy of one species but not know much about another. They will probably admit this if you ask them. I knew a Western guide who occasionally made decoys in the wintertime. One day when I was sitting by the stove in his shop watching him put the finishing touches on some hen canvasback, I complimented him on his decoys. He looked up from his painting with a grin and said, "They're all right. They'll ride in a hell of a blow on the lake, but they aren't worth a damn in a current. Move a mile from the lake to the mouth of the river where there's a three-mile-an-hour drag and they'll flip over and cut the cussedest capers you ever saw."

I asked if he knew why and he replied, "Nope! Don't care a damn, neither. Never shoot in the river m'self."

Inexperienced duck hunters will obviously have to seek local advice about where to shoot and which varieties of duck and geese use the area, and they may well profit by asking about decoys and where to buy them. However, they must be sure the information on decoys is up to date. They should guard against the point of view expressed by a Mississippi River gunner of my acquaintance who justified his rig by saying, "These were my dad's decoys and he killed thousands of duck over them. He was probably the best shot anywhere around here. These decoys were good enough for him and they sure are good enough for me."

My friend does not kill many duck over them. They were undoubtedly fine decoys by the standards of fifty years ago, but they are not comparable to those he could buy today. Since his father was evidently a skillful hunter, I think he would be quick to recognize the advantages to be gained by using new decoys if he were alive today. He probably once shot black powder in Damascus barrels, but I doubt if he continued to do so when smokeless powders and modern steel gun barrels came on the market.

7.

Activated Decoys

Bluebird days are viewed with disfavor by gunners because ducks, undisturbed by weather, do not fly as they do on meaner days; and when they do move on fair and windless days they do not decoy well. Duck hunters will find bluebird days less of a handicap if they will give their decoys some motion. In calm weather one or two *feeders* will give life to an entire rig and a *swimmer* will attract the attention of ducks at considerable distance. Every gunner has had the experience of seeing the V wake of a swimming duck before the duck itself was visible. This can be simulated with a well-rigged swimmer decoy and I know of no other device that pays such handsome dividends in ducks brought into range.

Motion of the water is the telltale sign of ducks feeding. Near my home is a small, brushy woodland pond which I pass on my way to a favorite grouse cover. There is always a chance of jumping a few ducks. There is a high bank along one side and the trick is to sneak up close enough to scan the surface for motion, sure evidence of ducks on the pond. If they did not move and stir up the water I would never spot them in the dense cover.

Bill Philips churned up the water by thrusting a paddle through an opening in the floor of his blind when birds were in the air. Another guide kept a bucket of small stones in his blind and he would surreptitiously throw a handful overside when he wanted to create a commotion in the water. A Vermonter with whom I shot had a marsh blind that gave wonderful protection to the hunters. He would shove his booted foot out the concealed door of the blind and kick up some waves on calm days when ducks were approaching. He said, "Little splashin' lends the hull rig a sartin versumilatude."

They are specialists at animating decoys down in the "pin oak" country along the lower Mississippi. They are much more likely than we up North to use feeder decoys or, as they say, "swing a boot or do suthin' to keep them stool a-movin' round." In Arkansas some guides use an elaborate contrivance that involves a big anchored paddle moved by a rope pulled from the blind and a stiff spring, attached to the paddle, which causes a backward sweep when the rope is released. The waves created by this paddie keep all their decoys in motion and they actually call the machine an *activator*.

Figures 2, 3, 4, and 5 show how to rig feeder and swimmer decoys. It is essential that your anchors be heavy, so that you can haul your swimmer in and out or up-end your feeder without dragging them toward you. If the anchors do not have weight enough they will move toward your blind with each pull on the line and will require constant resetting. Three or four of your standard anchors can be used instead of special anchors cast for these rigs. In order to keep your lines under water and concealed as much as possible it is wise to use one or two other heavy anchors with guides for your lines. Instead of blocks or pulleys, I now use brass rings about two inches in diameter made fast to the anchors and find the lines get fouled up less frequently when run through these. If the rings are not tarnished and inconspicuous they should be painted and your hauling lines must be a neutral color.

One line only is needed from the feeder to the blind, getting action by pulling hard enough on the line so that the forward part of your decoy is pulled under water, causing its tail to stick up in the air. Release the line suddenly so that the stern drops back into the water with quite a splash. A little practice will enable you to handle your decoy so it looks much like a feeding duck. Be sure the under side of the feeder decoy is properly painted. Your feeder will serve two purposes: beside resembling a feeding duck, the motion created on the water will give nearby decoys some action that they lack on calm days.

For the swimmer you have to run a double line so that you can haul your decoy out and have it ready to start swimming in toward your rig whenever ducks appear. Until you get the hang of handling these lines, you may have some difficulty with their fouling. But keep at it, for until you have tried out these activated decoys you will have no idea how much they will add to the effectiveness of your rig. I have found it expedient to separate the lines for manipulating the swimmer by the use of two inshore anchors or leads, as shown in Figure 3. In this way you avoid the likelihood of having your lines foul.

Both feeders and swimmers attract birds in moderate weather as well as in flat calm. In my experience those who have feeder decoys continue to use them and find them effective unless the wind is hard enough to kick up so much sea that their action becomes unnoticeable. Swimmers decoy best in a flat or almost-flat calm. Incidentally, there is no set formula for how far out to rig your swimmer. A number of local factors such as depth of water and type of bottom will have to be considered before rigging. One hundred yards from the blind is not too far if you can manage it. The swimmer does not have to move far or fast, just fast enough to create a visible wake, for it is the wake rather than the movement of the decoy that draws ducks' attention. If conditions compel you to "swim" your decoy a relatively short distance, leave an opening when you rig to enable you to take full advantage of whatever travel area you have—as suggested in Figure 5.

Few of today's duck hunters have ever shot over live decoys and therefore they do not feel the lack of them. The old-timers strive to create lifelike rigs, and even when live decoys could be

RIGGING A FEEDER DECOY

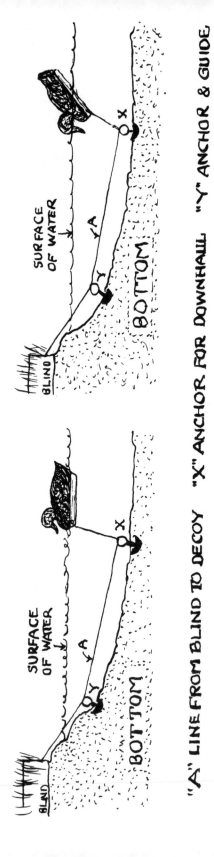

"A" LINE FROM BLIND TO DECOY   "X" ANCHOR FOR DOWNHAUL   "Y" ANCHOR & GUIDE

FIGURE 2

Rigging a Swimming Decoy

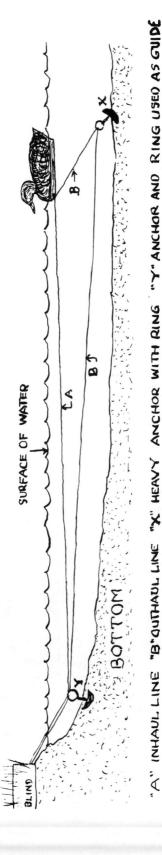

SURFACE OF WATER

BOTTOM

X

Y

B →

B ↑

A ↑

BLIND

FIGURE 3

"A" INHAUL LINE "B" OUTHAUL LINE "X" HEAVY ANCHOR WITH RING "Y" ANCHOR AND RING USED AS GUIDE

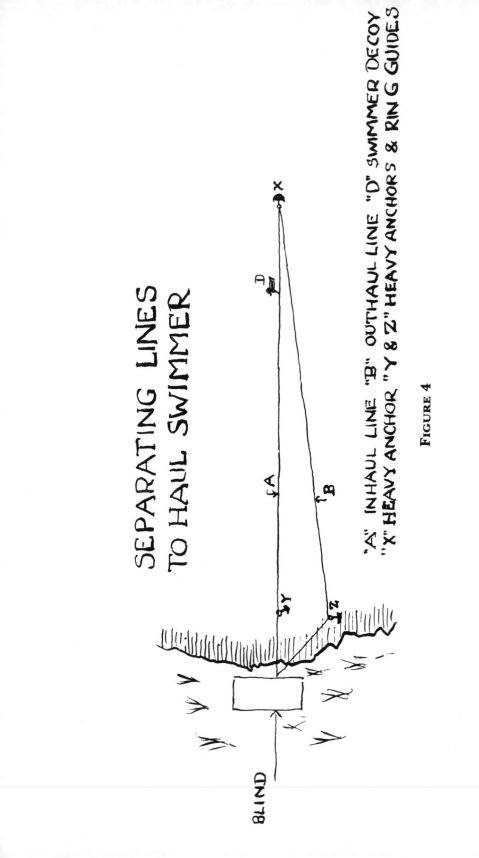

SEPARATING LINES
TO HAUL SWIMMER

"A" INHAUL LINE "B" OUTHAUL LINE "D" SWIMMER DECOY
"X" HEAVY ANCHOR "Y & Z" HEAVY ANCHORS & RING GUIDES

FIGURE 4

BLIND

MAKE ROOM IN RIG FOR SWIMMER DECOY

WIND ⟶

X   OUTER ANCHOR
Y & Z   ANCHORED GUIDES
A   INHAUL LINE
B   OUTHAUL LINE
D   SWIMMER DECOY
W   WAKE

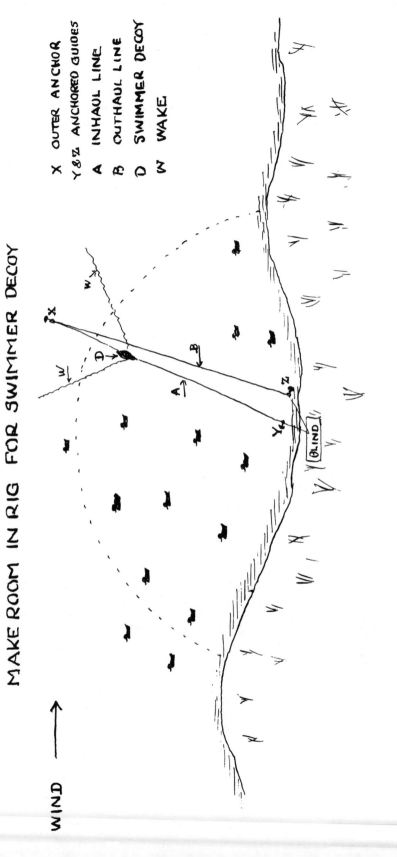

BLIND

FIGURE 5

used some of them preferred activated wooden decoys. Charles DoVille, with whom I shot on Lake Ontario when I was a boy, was a master of animation. He rigged swimmers and feeders and actually made and used decoys that would flap their wings. There was nothing lifeless about his rig. The more experienced gunner is the first to recognize the need for such helps as activated decoys and good duck calls. The thinner the shooting and the less auspicious the day, the more important these imitations of natural birds become. There are generally a few days in each duck season when due to weather almost anyone can kill a limit. Since many of us cannot arrange to go shooting on just those top days, but must take our weather as it comes along, it pays to emulate the experts and learn how to activate our decoys.

8.

Anchors, Lines, and Anchoring

Nowhere in the entire field of wildfowling is wider choice displayed than in the selection of anchors. Depth of water, type of bottom, exposure to wind or current, method of storing, and means of transportation are some of the things that influence the decision. Some of the least orthodox solutions are frequently the best. A crotched stick cut "on the job" with the anchor line tied to it before it is pushed into the soft bottom by a booted foot serves ideally under the right conditions. A guide in Louisiana stopped in the dark one morning before we got to the blind where we were going to shoot, and gathered half a sack of broken bricks at an abandoned brick yard—perfect anchors in that particular situation. These improvisations are mentioned only to suggest that ingenious gunners have thought of methods to avoid toting heavy loads of anchors to places where some expendable substitute can be easily had.

Transportation enters into the choice of anchors. If from the beginning to the end of the season your decoys can safely stay in your duck boat or your blind, you have little concern with the weight of anchors. On the other hand, if you are like most of us you will be moving decoys from woodshed to car, car to dock, and dock to boat—and any weight considered surplus is to be avoided. I suggest you explore the possibilities of mooring a

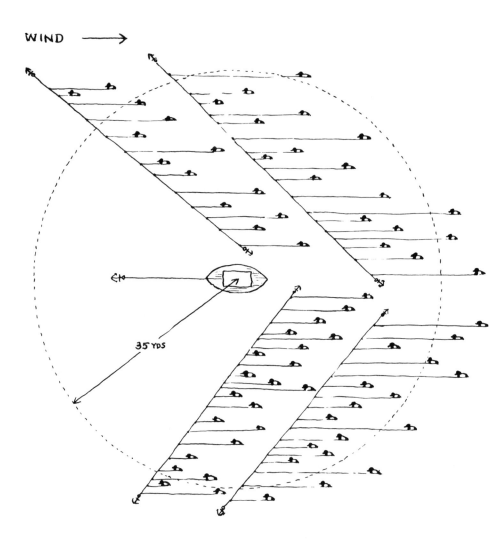

WIND →

35 YDS

MULTIPLE RIGGING OF
FOUR LINES OF DECOYS
AROUND LAYOUT BOAT

FIGURE 6

number of decoys to a single line anchored at each end. This statement will probably bring howls of protest from the "anchor-them-one-at-a-time" boys, of which group I am normally a strong supporting member. I veer from the straight and narrow when the avoidance of weight becomes important or I may have to shift large groups of decoys during the day. Some experimenting with the lengths of line used to make individual decoys fast to the single anchor line can achieve fairly good results as the drawings show.

Decoy anchors have been developed over the years along three general lines—the mushroom anchor, the grapnel, and those that serve the added purpose of holding the line, shaped to fit over a decoy's head. In deep water and on rocky ledges sometimes only a grapnel will hold, but by far the most popular and widely used anchor is some form of the mushroom. The horseshoe or loop-type anchor is handy to slip over your decoy's head, but because of its smooth surfaces it will not hold as well as a mushroom of the same weight. Whether you buy anchors, cast them yourself, or have them cast locally, be sure they are adequate to hold your decoys on the type of bottom where you shoot.

Decoys ride best at anchor if the lines are made fast to them with a swivel. Most swivels are made so that anchor lines can be easily detached.

Hy Dahlka, who shoots in the western end of Lake Erie off Pointe Mouilee, has been converted to multiple rigging after years of anchoring his rigs of canvasback and redhead singly. He told me he now uses groups of fifteen or sixteen decoys on one line anchored at both ends. The entire rig of more than one hundred decoys can be picked up by two men and relocated in fifteen minutes, and under the conditions in which he shoots this is sometimes necessary several times a day. An end decoy is picked up, the anchor pulled in and hung on a hook in the power boat that serves as a tender for his rigs. The lines are coiled down as they are hauled aboard, the decoys set in a row on the cockpit floor, and the second anchor is hung on another

[41]

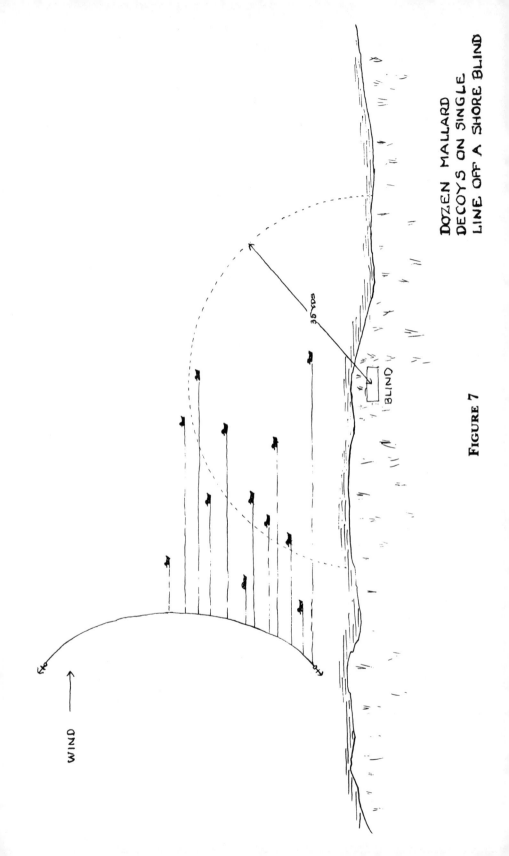

DOZEN MALLARD
DECOYS ON SINGLE
LINE OFF A SHORE BLIND

BLIND

35 YDS

WIND

FIGURE 7

hook. Dahlka claims that he has seen no evidence that ducks are less willing to come in to the multiple rigging. He says that apparently ducks haven't studied geometry and cannot tell the difference between a circle and a triangle. Actually, the decoys are not strung out in parallel lines—due to his skillful placing of the two anchors.

In moderate weather I anchor about half my decoys so they ride stern first. This helps to avoid the "alert" look that comes when decoys are all headed upwind. In heavy weather ducks tend to ride headed into the wind and so should decoys. It is wise to lengthen anchor lines in heavy weather. A light anchor will hold better if the pull of the line is nearly parallel to the bottom, thereby averting the tendency for it to lift each time a sea picks the decoy up. In a really hard blow when decoys were beginning to drift, a guide once saved the situation by taking the line off one decoy, combining the two anchors and tying the two lines together, keeping only enough to fasten one decoy astern of the other. The combined anchors with the longer line held, and in the heavy sea it did not matter that our decoys were all riding as pairs.

It is difficult to buy good anchor line and I am still experimenting. Lines of the proper color are often too light in weight, are too stiff to handle, or lack strength. Sources for anchor lines are the outfitters who supply commercial fishermen or sporting-goods stores where you should find soft, strong, dark-colored fishline.

The color of anchor line is more important than many gunners realize. I have seen a good rig rendered ineffective by the use of near-white lines that made an odd and obviously unattractive pattern when viewed from above. Ducks coming in overhead can see under water clearly and at quite a distance. Many details, such as the color of anchor lines, are less important in heavy weather but become of critical importance and make the difference between success and failure in moderate weather.

[43]

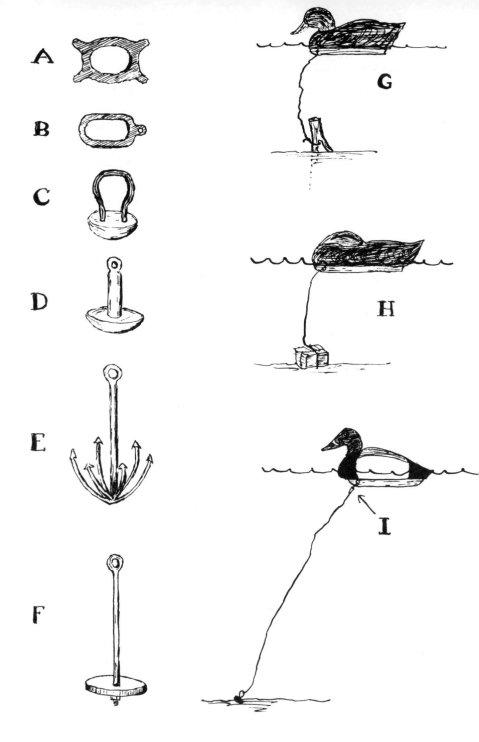

A & B OVER THE HEAD ANCHORS   C & D MUSHROOMS
E GRAPNEL   F DAHLKA ANCHOR   G "STICK IN
THE MUD" H BRICK   I SWIVEL IN LINE

FIGURE 8

9.

Blinds

Stewart Edward White once pointed out that the word *camp* lends itself to a variety of concepts, ranging, in his experience, from an elaborate, servant-haunted structure built of stone and logs to one without a fire on the lee side of a prairie rock that kept some of the cold rain off his single blanket. This is also true of the word *blind*. It can be anything that provides effective concealment. The simplest blinds I have ever seen were pieces of light canvas covered with blue-gray paint that matched the color of a rocky point. We lay down, pulled the canvas over us, and propped up one corner with a stick so that we could peek out toward our decoys. When birds came in we threw back the canvas, sat up, and shot. A white sheet or sail used in the same way when the shore is covered with snow gives excellent protection, and a layout boat painted white with the gunners wearing white coveralls will work well when ice has formed along a channel.

In complete reversal of this simplicity, I have enjoyed fine shooting from a "houseboat" on Lake Champlain which was the most elaborate blind I ever saw. It was the only survivor of a type common on that lake many years ago. I have included two drawings of this outfit; it was amazingly comfortable and efficient and I see no reason why it might not be duplicated

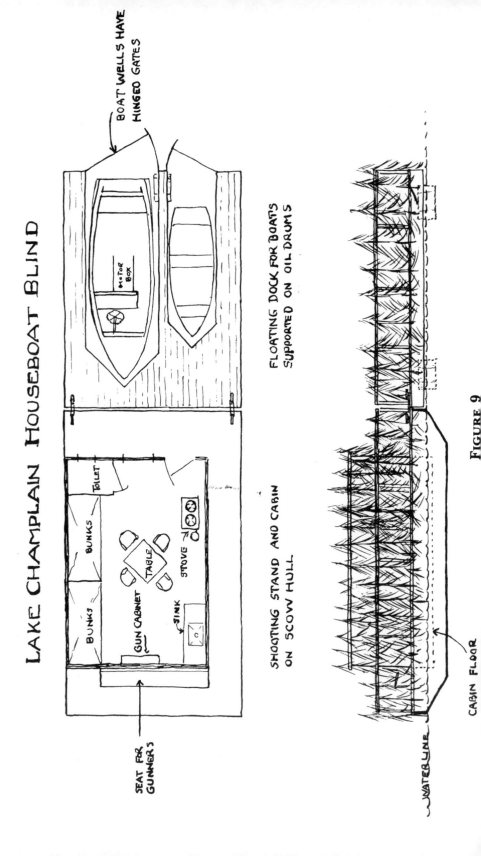

LAKE CHAMPLAIN HOUSEBOAT BLIND

BOAT WELLS HAVE HINGED GATES

MOTOR BOX

FLOATING DOCK FOR BOATS SUPPORTED ON OIL DRUMS

SEAT FOR GUNNERS

TOILET

BUNKS

BUNKS

GUN CABINET

TABLE

SINK

C

STOVE

SHOOTING STAND AND CABIN ON SCOW HULL

WATER LINE

CABIN FLOOR

FIGURE 9

elsewhere, providing the location is good enough and the amount of time it could be used justified its cost.

In order that the general outline of this floating palace may be seen, the camouflage is only faintly suggested in the drawing. Actually the sides were thoroughly screened with fresh-cut cedar branches nailed to the rail around the edge of the scow, to the sides of the cabin, and around the boat-wells at the back. Cut cedars were thrown on the cabin roof and a few were thrown in the boats.

The owner of this elaborate shooting device said of it, "It's so damned big the ducks must think it's an island covered with cedar trees. There are plenty in the lake and the ducks aren't bothered by another island."

As the plan indicates, there were wells for a power boat and a skiff and these were enclosed by water gates hinged to the extended sides of the float. In the cabin were a pair of double bunks, a table and four chairs, a cook stove, and a toilet. The owner could run down the lake in time for the late-afternoon shooting, cook dinner and sleep aboard, have a crack at the early-morning flight, and then pull out in the power boat to be back at work at his usual time. Few of us are so well situated with our home and our business within a few miles of good duck shooting, but the houseboat offers something remarkable in convenience, comfort, and concealment for the man with both the days and the dollars.

For the successful use of any conspicuous and semipermanent blind, like the houseboat or big stake blinds, three conditions must be met. The blinds should be built or anchored long before the start of the season so that ducks become accustomed to them and accept them as a natural part of the landscape. They ought to be located in areas where ducks feed or normally use and they must not be overshot. In fact, there should be more rest days than days with shooting.

In various sections of the country stake blinds are favored. They are usually constructed well in advance of the season by driving stakes or piles into the bottom of lakes, bayous, or

[49]

PLAN OF STAKE BLIND

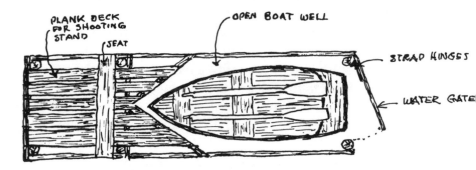

PLANK DECK FOR SHOOTING STAND — OPEN BOAT WELL — STRAP HINGES — SEAT — WATER GATE

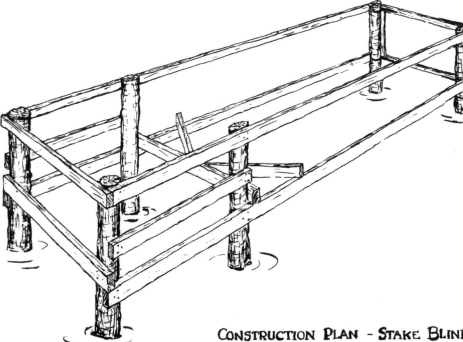

CONSTRUCTION PLAN - STAKE BLIND
SHOWING FRAMING BEFORE FLOOR IS LAID OR ANY CAMOUFLAGE IS APPLIED

FIGURE 10

FLOATING BLINDS
ARE FREQUENTLY
CARRIED ON LOGS

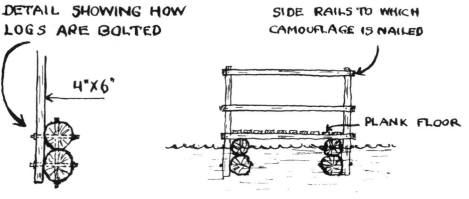

DETAIL SHOWING HOW
LOGS ARE BOLTED

4"X6"

SIDE RAILS TO WHICH
CAMOUFLAGE IS NAILED

PLANK FLOOR

FRONT VIEW

FLOATING BLIND CARRIED ON OIL DRUMS

FIGURE 11

rivers. The stakes are tied together with stringers usually just above the waterline and again at the top of the rail or fence marking the top of the blind. A platform is built at one end as a shooting stand and an open well is left for the boat in back of this. The blind is thoroughly thatched with cattails, cedar, or some other local and natural cover, the rear of the boat-well being closed by a water gate hinged on one side and also thoroughly covered with thatch. A variant calls for flooring the entire blind and building it high enough so the boat is housed under the platform. This has the advantage of allowing the gunners to face easily in any direction from which ducks may come, but the disadvantage of requiring the whole structure to stand much higher.

Floating blinds are quite similar to stake blinds. Big logs are spiked or bolted together to make floats. Oil drums with a frame built around them are also used. A float bracket has been developed, making it easy to securely fasten wooden frames to fifty-five-gallon drums. While these were intended for landing floats and docks, they are ideal for use in making floating blinds. Since they can be simply "unbolted" at the end of a season, they aid in the chore of getting the blind ashore for winter storage. Uprights are fastened to the floats and tied together at the top, as they are in stake blinds, and similarly thatched. In some of these blinds a platform is built with a boat-well behind it exactly as in stake blinds. In others, especially smaller blinds, semisubmerged cross-stringers partially support the boat in which the gunners sit. A heavy anchor is made fast with a bridle to the bow to keep the blind in place, and a lighter stern anchor, which can be easily lifted and moved, controls the position in which the blind lies in relation to the wind and seas.

In these blinds, in all types of blinds for that matter, overhead camouflage is most often neglected. It is important to carry the thatching up so that it tends to blend in, concealing the gunners from ducks flying high above them.

If the water level and the nature of the shore permit digging into the ground, there is no finer type of blind for pond or

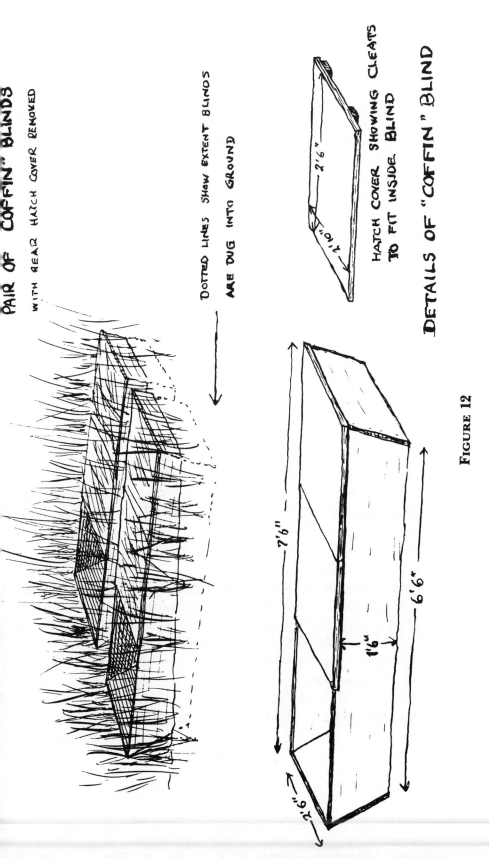

PAIR OF "COFFIN" BLINDS

WITH REAR HATCH COVER REMOVED

DOTTED LINES SHOW EXTENT BLINDS

ARE DUG INTO GROUND

2'6"

1'0"

HATCH COVER SHOWING CLEATS
TO FIT INSIDE BLIND

DETAILS OF "COFFIN" BLIND

7'6"

6'6"

1'6"

2'6"

FIGURE 12

point shooting than the lay-down or coffin blind illustrated in Figure 12. Properly built and with natural cover left around them, these are unquestionably the best blinds for low-marsh or salt-meadow shooting. It is customary to have three hatch covers over each blind, one of which is removed so the gunner slides down into the box which is lined with straw. Grass is wired flat on the top of the hatch covers to add to the camouflage. The gunner lies down much as he would in a layout boat, his gun being placed on the remaining hatch covers before him— safe and ready. Sometimes as many as four of these blinds are located alongside each other, and if the grass is left standing between them or screens of grass are made to separate them they still provide excellent concealment. Properly built, screened, and dug in, they are difficult to spot fifty yards away, even when you know where to look for them.

Figure 13 shows the plan of a floating blind usually anchored against or near a marsh island or marshy shore. It has an advantage over a similar outfit built on shore in that it can be moved to a new location when changing weather or flight conditions require it. On tidewater these blinds, or some other floating blinds, are almost essential because of the changing water levels. This floating blind is built on a scow sixteen feet long, seven feet wide, and two feet deep, decked over for two feet on each end and for a foot and a half along the sides (leaving a cockpit four by twelve). A floor is carried on three two-by-sixes set on edge and running the length of the hull. A coaming is built up from this floor to a height of four feet. The bottom planking is nailed to these stringers. An eighteen-inch rail is carried around the outer edge of the deck except where the two-foot deck areas on each end are left open at the back for entry to the blind. This rail is connected to the top of the blind by chicken wire into which bunches of grass are thrust, and the blind proper, the scow, and the rail are thatched with grass.

A seat runs along the back of the blind, and two shelves run the full length of the front. The upper shelf is covered with grass fastened flat as camouflage. It extends beyond the lower

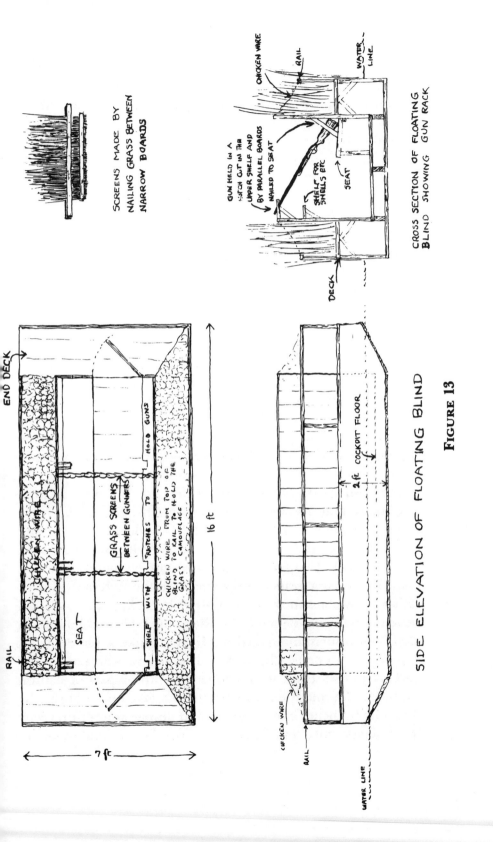

SCREENS MADE BY NAILING GRASS BETWEEN NARROW BOARDS

GUN HELD IN A NOTCH CUT IN THE UPPER SHELF AND BY PARALLEL BOARDS NAILED TO SEAT

CHICKEN WIRE

RAIL

WATER LINE

SHELF FOR SHELLS ETC.

SEAT

DECK

CROSS SECTION OF FLOATING BLIND SHOWING GUN RACK

END DECK

RAIL

CHICKEN WIRE

SEAT

GRASS SCREENS BETWEEN GUNNERS

SHELF WITH NOTCHES TO HOLD GUNS

CHICKEN WIRE FROM TOP OF BLIND TO RAIL TO HOLD THE GRASS CAMOUFLAGE

7 ft

16 ft

2 ft COCKPIT FLOOR

CHICKEN WIRE

RAIL

WATER LINE

SIDE ELEVATION OF FLOATING BLIND

FIGURE 13

shelf which serves as a handy storage space for shells, thermos bottles, etc. Hatches are cut in the floor to permit bailing and a canvas cover to keep rain water out is buttoned over the cockpit when the blind is not in use. In Figure 5 the grass dividers made by nailing grass between four pieces of lath are shown. These fit between the gunners' positions to break up what would otherwise be an open view of the blind to ducks coming in from the side. The doors in the coaming at the ends of the blind are shown in the drawing, but these are heavily thatched to close the ends of the blind to view. A small drawing gives the details of the gun racks which hold the guns upright and in a ready position. In extreme weather the gunners in these blinds can be kept remarkably warm by the use of a pair of old-fashioned, round oil stoves, or just an ordinary farm lantern for each man will do the job.

Natural cover where nothing need be added except perhaps an up-ended shell box to sit on makes the best possible blind. The duck hunter is fortunate if he can conceal himself behind bushes or in tall pampas grass, reeds, or rushes and set his decoys where they will bring ducks within range. His only concern should be not to break down his cover or let a clearly defined path or entry expose his hide-out.

The best place to locate a blind depends so much on local conditions that no specific advice can be given, but some generalities should be kept in mind. Ducks do not like to swing to decoys over land, nor will they decoy well close in under a bank or bluff. Temporary blinds (or portable blinds) are best made by weaving grass or other material through old fishnets, rather than chicken wire, supported by stakes. The material woven into the net depends on what is available and how it will blend with surrounding cover. If you build a blind on an exposed shore or beach, work it in somehow with part of the background so it will seem connected with or part of natural cover. Build a rough fence or construct a fake row of bushes by thrusting branches into the ground. If despite your efforts your blind stands out from its surroundings like a lighthouse, try erecting some similar structures nearby. Three or four odd additions to the landscape, only one of which is used, are less disturbing apparently than a single fortress.

Blinds are built low, if possible, in relation to nearby cover. Toward the end of a season after ducks have been much shot at, the combination of a rig of decoys and a conspicuous blind is likely to frighten birds instead of attracting them. Ducks get wary of blinds from which they have taken a pounding, and this causes them to behave in an unpredictable manner.

A few years ago, shooting with an architect friend near the Canadian border, we were using adjoining stone blinds of the kind peculiar to the St. Lawrence River Valley. The weather was theoretically ideal—cold with a wind of near-gale force. Duck were plentiful and were moving near us, but they would not come into our rig. They would swing toward us, but when about two gunshots out they would turn away. This maddening performance continued for hours while the thermometer dropped steadily. Stone blinds were never noted for their warmth and I finally got so cold that I went back from the water's edge perhaps seventy-five feet, gathered some wood, and lit a fire. When it was blazing nicely I called my companion to come and get warm.

We were in plain sight with a brisk fire burning and he had hardly reached the blaze when four mallards sat down among our decoys. We attempted to sneak back to the blinds and our guns, but of course the ducks jumped before we got there. We promptly doused the fire and got back into the blinds. Nothing happened. The duck kept their previous distance. After an hour passed we decided to get warm and built another fire. Again the ducks came in to our decoys as soon as we were out of the blinds. We left the fire burning and sat down in plain sight near the blinds. As long as we kept perfectly still the ducks decoyed and we had good shooting.

The explanation seems quite clear. The ducks had learned to watch these blinds and the slightest motion in them was a danger signal. In an effort to keep an eye on flying ducks, looking through different chinks in the blinds, we were moving and giving ourselves away. The fire was not a factor. It gave us a chance to thaw out once in a while, but the ducks had not learned to connect it with danger. I am sure it would not take them many days to do so.

An excellent blind can be made ineffective by visible motion or wrong colors. Colors contrasting sharply with the background are to be avoided, bright red and white seem to be the most "scary." Red is for deer hunting. Make sure that no colorful ejected shells are exposed with their brass bases reflecting the sun. Remember the number of times you have spotted an empty shell near a blind or in a marsh and commented on it? Give the ducks credit for better eyesight than you have.

Unless there is snow on the ground do not use white. Anything white, big or little, a boat or a handkerchief, is to be avoided. A fine guide, Charles Bussanih, was always conscious of color and was quick to comment on any part of his customer's clothing or equipment of which he disapproved. Shooting with him in Shinnecock Bay, we once had an interesting proof of the effect of color. After two or three hours of good shooting, ducks abruptly stopped coming in to our decoys. They continued to move up and down the bay, but gave our decoys a wide berth. We were shooting over a hard sand bottom and could wade out to set decoys or pick up our kill. After half an hour of this shooting lull, Charlie got out of the blind, waded out among the decoys, and studied the layout and particuarly the blind. He finally climbed back in saying, "Damn' if I can see anything wrong. Wind's the same, light's the same, but the duck see something they don't like. Maybe you fellers are sitting too high. Scrouge down more and keep down."

No result. The birds still passed us by. Charlie then walked around the blind, looked for empty shells, threw more grass over the birds we had killed which were piled up back of the blind, again he waded out among the decoys to survey the scene. On his way in he picked up an empty cigarette box one of us had thrown out and tucked it under some grass on shore. He did this automatically, I'm sure, rather than with a sense that this box under a foot of water was flaring the birds, but that was it. Duck again decoyed well.

10.

Rigging Shore Blinds

Market gunners and old-time guides, who gunned every day of seasons five times longer than ours, had great opportunity to watch ducks decoying or, if they failed to decoy, to study and correct the faults of their rigs. Their livelihood depended on "getting the birds in." They learned by trial and error how best to rig and how to move their rigs when conditions changed and birds did not come in to them. I have had the good fortune to gun with some of them and with their sons and grandsons who have inherited some of their lore.

A good many years ago I shot on a New England tidal marsh with Captain Billy Rand, an old market-gunner-turned-guide, typical of his kind. The old man—he actually was in his eighties—at first seemed slow and doddering, but I kept going back because we had good luck, or so it appeared. Finally I began to appreciate him. Some mornings we would be rigged out an hour before sunup, but usually he would sit on a high point behind the marsh and watch for ducks to move. "Be just as good sittin' here till we know where they're usin'," he would say. Sometimes it was past noon before he would pick a location. There might not be a bird in the air while he rigged out, but when questioned he would answer, "Be knockin' our hats off in an hour or so."

This shrewd guide set his decoys with great care. After rigging them, he would let his boat drift downwind a couple of hundred yards and study the set. Sometimes he would approve, but he was more likely to row back and move a few decoys. The finishing touch was a pair of black duck decoys set close together a hundred yards downwind from the others. He then set a lone white sea gull decoy upwind at the head of the rig. The only comment he offered about the pair of decoys below the rig was that they "kinda bring 'em in lower." About the gull decoy his explanation was simple. "Never see a gull light in with your decoys, did yuh? Well, they light in with ducks when there ain't a blind there. Makes it look safer to the ducks, I figure."

We cannot acquire parallel knowledge of local conditions, of the way birds "use" in that marsh, since we cannot hope to match Captain Rand's sixty-five years of gunning there—something more than five thousand days of duck shooting any way you figure it. We can add his sea gull and his hundred-yards-away pair to our rigs.

Joe Dawson, one of the most proficient men with decoys I have known, had several gunning stands on the tidewater creeks running into Chesapeake Bay. He was a specialist gunning for mallard duck and occasionally for geese. He made his own decoys, remarkably good ones, and in his area knew exactly how to rig. We had fair shooting one day from one of his blinds until two gunners arrived to rig in a blind just off the edge of his property and about two hundred and fifty yards downwind from us along the same creek. "That'll fix it," said Joe. "They'll get all the birds."

They did for an hour, then he climbed out of the blind and started for his boat, saying, "They've had enough. I'll be back."

He returned a bit later with a lone goose decoy in his boat. He set it on the far side of the creek fifty yards downwind from our decoys and about two hundred yards from the other blind. He rowed up the creek, left his boat hidden, and climbed back into the blind. I was completely mystified and asked what the goose was for. Joe chuckled and said, "You watch the ducks. We'll get and they won't."

[62]

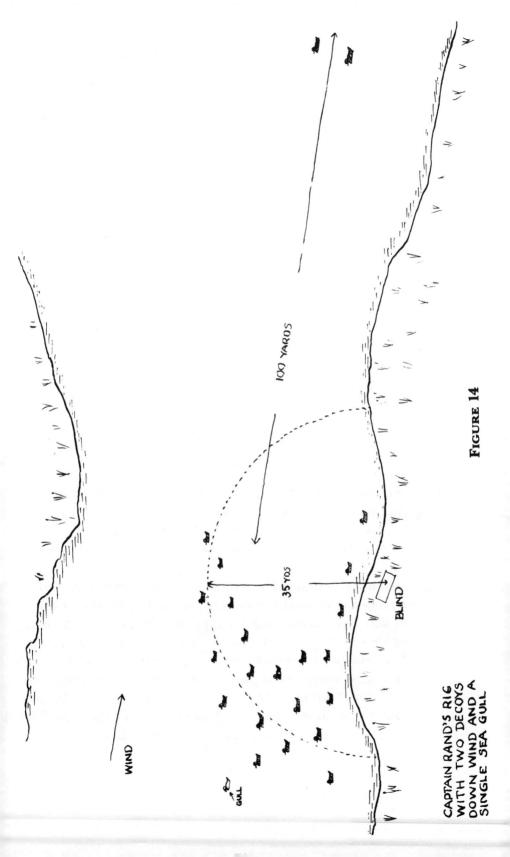

WIND

100 YARDS

35 YDS

BLIND

GULL

CAPTAIN RAND'S RIG
WITH TWO DECOYS
DOWN WIND AND A
SINGLE SEA GULL

FIGURE 14

Our shooting was not as good as it had been early in the morning before the other gunners rigged, but after Joe set the goose decoy the other blind never had a shot. Ducks would flare before they got within their range, but some turned in to our decoys. Joe either could not or would not explain the effect of the goose decoy except to say, "Them birds see the goose just before they get to their rig and they swing to see what else is up the creek. Then they see our rig and some keep a-comin'."

Many of the old-timers handled the details of their gunning instinctively rather than thoughtfully. They knew a particular spread of decoys was right for certain locations or conditions, but they had difficulty in explaining how they knew. A Louisiana guide put goose silhouettes around a pit on a Mississippi sand bar on the expressed theory that the wind would come hard out of the east before sundown and geese would fly late in the day. When proved right, he was asked how he knew. Pointing overhead at a flight of gulls heading north against the sunset sky, he asked us, "How does they's gulls know 'bout gettin' back from way out yondah in the Gu'f?"

I have asked questions and made sketches and whiled away bluebird days talking decoys and how to rig them. I have a drawer full of sketches, mostly made with blunt pencils on ruled paper, sent me by some of these old-timers to prove a point or answer an inquiry. I have learned, of course, there is no single right way to rig, no golden formula. There are some fundamentals to be learned and there are a few rather solid *don'ts*.

I have seen decoys dumped overboard or tossed indiscriminately through the air and left all day wherever they were thrown, without regard to changes in wind or current. Conditions have to be perfect and birds plentiful to produce shooting when decoys are handled that way. The *first rule* of rigging is to make a plan after carefully surveying the situation where you are going to shoot—then place your decoys exactly where you want them. Nothing is surer to spoil a good start for a day's shooting than to get into your blind and find, when wind or current have straightened out your anchor lines, that your

[64]

decoys are bunched together unnaturally or drifted too far out or too close in. Make a plan. Take your time. Rig with care. If bad weather or a late start makes you hurry your rigging, rig fewer decoys, to save time, but rig them well.

The *second rule* of rigging is to change your rig if conditions change. *Again,* make a plan for the new situation and take time to place your decoys where they will best serve you. The beginner may well ask how often changes should be made and the answer is as often as conditions change. Fortunately it is unlikely that the wind will haul completely around several times during a day and force the complete relocation of the entire rig. It is more apt to haul a few points from east to southeast, for example, or from east to northeast. Moving a few decoys will frequently suffice in such cases. If, however, the wind really hauls from east to west, then a change to a new location or a complete rerigging is called for.

Gunners who have a choice of locations and can pick a blind suited to the conditions of the day are fortunate. Most of us are lucky if we have a single good spot from which to shoot and our problem becomes one of developing methods of rigging a fixed location to meet varying factors of weather and bird activity. East Island represents such a place and the six diagrams show how decoys were set for six different wind directions.

Despite fairly shoal water we found it desirable most of the time to rig for diving ducks as well as for geese and shoal-water ducks. On East Island a true east wind gave us our most difficult problem, since birds had to swing over the land and almost over our heads to reach the decoys. The two drawings showing rigs for northeast and southeast winds, if compared with the drawing showing the east-wind rig, serve to illustrate two things: (1) how much a wind change can affect shooting conditions, in each case changing the problem from a bad setup to a reasonably good one, and (2) how relatively little change in the rig was needed to compensate for these wind shifts. Our blinds on East Island were dug in, otherwise we certainly would have moved the entire rig on a true east wind. Incidentally

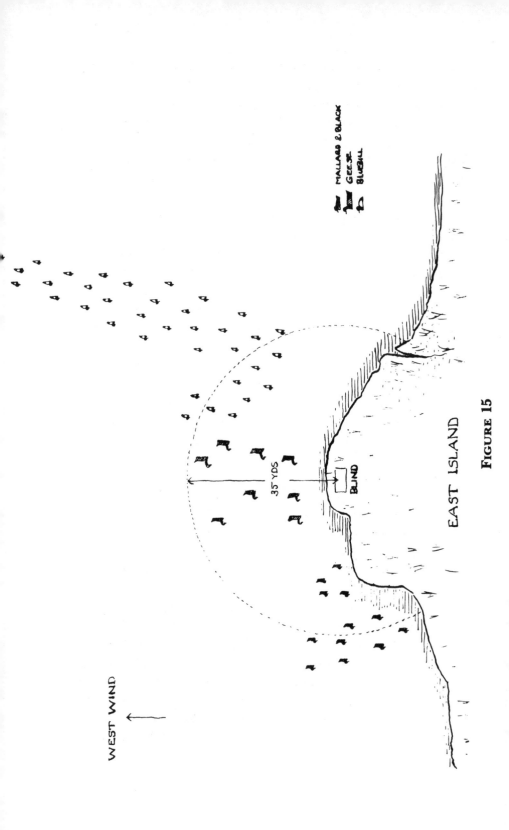

WEST WIND ←

35 YDS

BLIND

MALLARD & BLACK
GEESE
BLUEBILL

EAST ISLAND

FIGURE 15

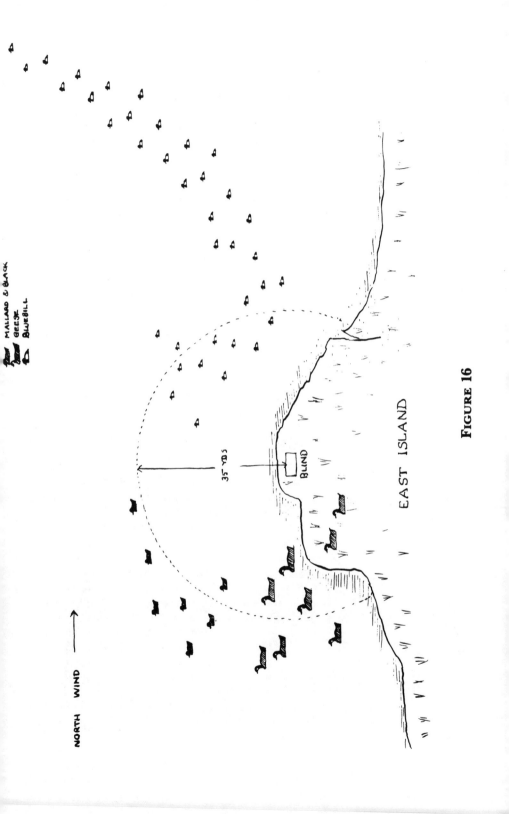

MALLARD & BLACK
GEESE
BLUEBILL

NORTH WIND

35 YDS

BLIND

EAST ISLAND

FIGURE 16

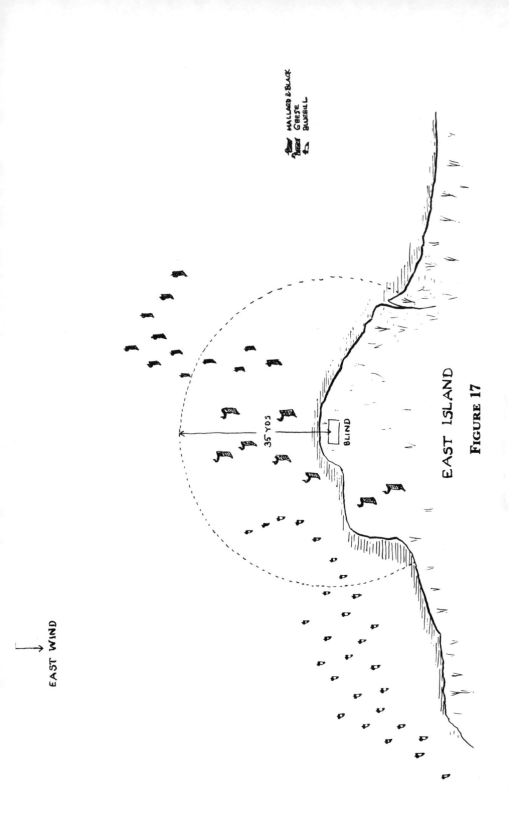

EAST WIND

MALLARD & BLACK
GEESE
BLUEBILL

35 YDS

BLIND

EAST ISLAND

FIGURE 17

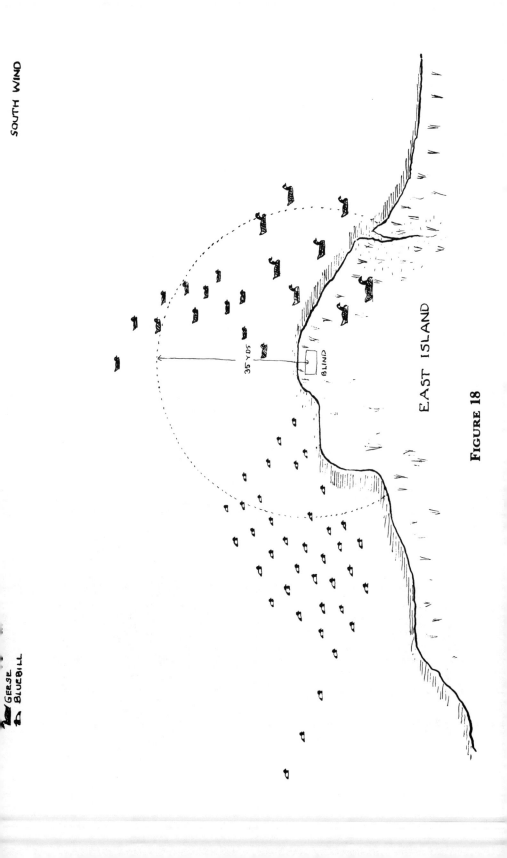

SOUTH WIND

GEESE
BLUEBILL

35 YDS

BLIND

EAST ISLAND

FIGURE 18

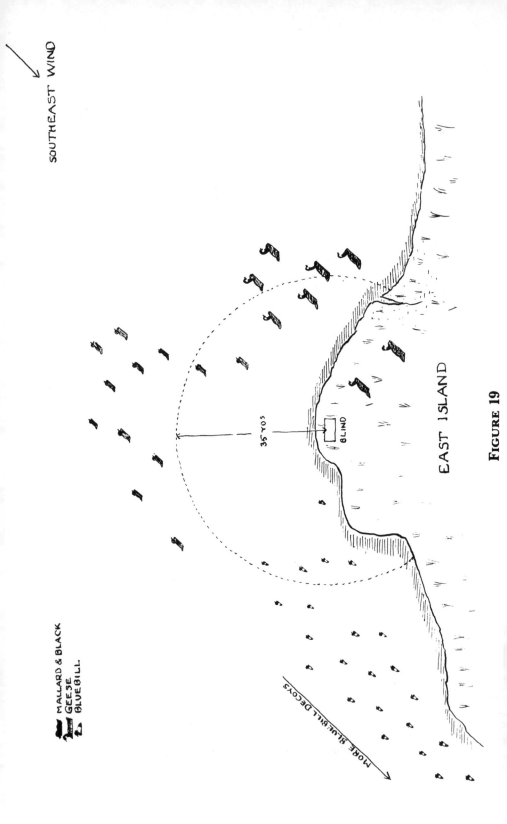

FIGURE 19

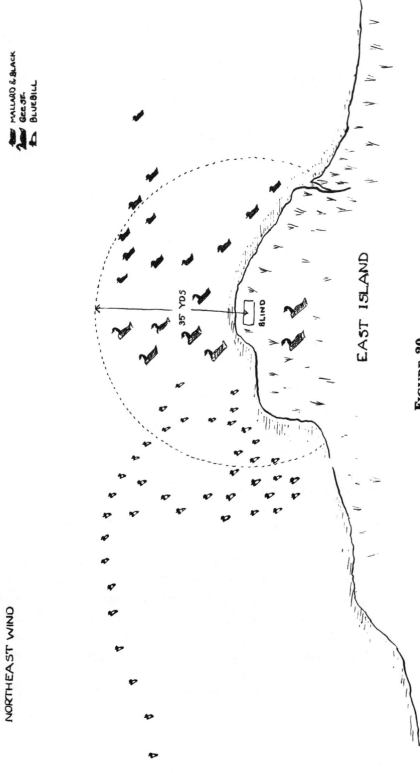

NORTHEAST WIND

MALLARD & BLACK
GEESE
BLUEBILL

35 YDS

BLIND

EAST ISLAND

FIGURE 20

these blinds were the coffin boxes shown in Chapter 9 which hide the gunner almost completely from birds, even when they are overhead. No blind open at the top would have served in this spot on an east wind.

This *second rule* of rigging, to change your rig when conditions change, is hard to remember. It is easy to sit in the blind because there are birds in the air or you think the wind will haul back again after lunch, or for some other equally invalid reason. We all tell of the times we were out changing the rig and a flight of duck "tried" to come in. What we do not tell is of the times we sat in the blind putting off the arduous chore of shifting the decoys and watched a big flight start for our decoys, but change their minds and depart for far places. It is better to have your rig right and get an hour or so of good shooting than to sit hopefully all day in a blind when duck decoy badly or not at all.

The *third basic rule* is to change your rig or at least determine what the trouble is when birds refuse to decoy. It may be movement in the blind, the glint of a gun barrel, or any one of a number of things having nothing to do with rigging; but it may be the fault of the rig. Figure it out and correct it. Get out in your boat and study your rig from the far side, from downwind. Get a duck's-eye view of the situation.

Don't wait, if duck do not behave as you wish, try to do something about it. An experience in the historic Saginaw River Marshes in Michigan illustrates the point. We were shooting in rain and a hard south blow. Louis and Jacques DuPraw used to say they could kill a duck a minute in this marsh when conditions were right. We were not doing quite that well—it was seventy years ago they shot there—but ducks had been decoying excellently when suddenly, for no reason we could fathom, they began to flare. No change in the weather had occurred. After a few ducks started for our decoys, then turned away, my host suggested we pole out, pick up our dead birds, and see if we could discover the trouble. He spotted one widgeon floating, white breast up, in the rushes at the edge of the pond. (See x on Figure 21.) This was twenty-five or thirty yards downwind from

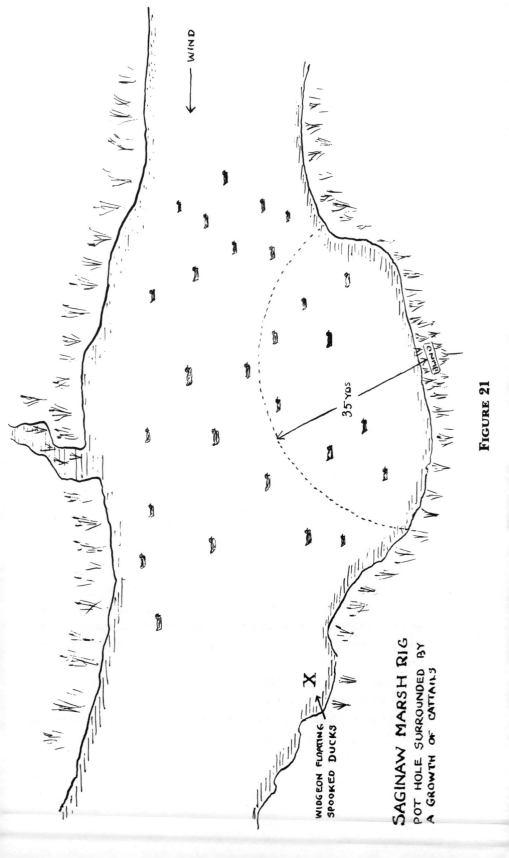

WIND

35-YDS

X

WIDGEON FLOATING
SPOOKED DUCKS

SAGINAW MARSH RIG
POT HOLE SURROUNDED BY
A GROWTH OF CATTAILS

FIGURE 21

our decoys, but nothing else seemed amiss. We picked this bird up with the rest of our kill and got back into the blind. That was it. The next ducks starting our way decoyed perfectly.

The diagram of the rig in the Housatonic River Marsh in Connecticut is in sharp contrast to the Saginaw Marsh layout, but the areas are not unlike. The particular channels through the marshes are about the same width and, except for the rise and fall of tides and the resulting currents in the Housatonic, they are remarkably parallel for gunning stands so widely separated. Both blinds are "naturals" and the gunners were concealed by native vegetation without added cover. Both were gunned exclusively by their owners, who shot only occasionally, providing plenty of "rest" time for the birds. They both gunned for the same birds: blacks, mallards, widgeon, pintail, and teal. Both were experts, students of local conditions, and they had arrived at completely different rigs by watching the behavior of ducks in their marshes. I have had superb shooting in both stands and I am convinced each of these gunners had achieved an almost perfect rig for his special conditions of feed and flight. A study of the two rigs should convince the average shooter of the need for keen observation and great care and thought in rigging. I am persuaded, despite the obvious sameness of many features of these gunning stands, that the rigs could not be transposed and work as well.

One blustery fall night aboard a houseboat on a Western lake I described a situation to a group of experienced gunners, drew rough pictures of a bay and sand bar on Lake Ontario where I sometimes shot, and asked for advice on rigging. This provoked a series of questions ranging from the depth of water to how much my canvasback decoys weighed, but produced little information. One of the experts finally picked up a pencil, drew a few tentative circles on my map to represent decoys, carefully erased them, shook his head, and said, "Don't know as I can tell you, but, by God, if we were there I could rig."

I am going to follow his example and avoid the hypothetical. The diagrams that accompany these chapters on rigging make

[74]

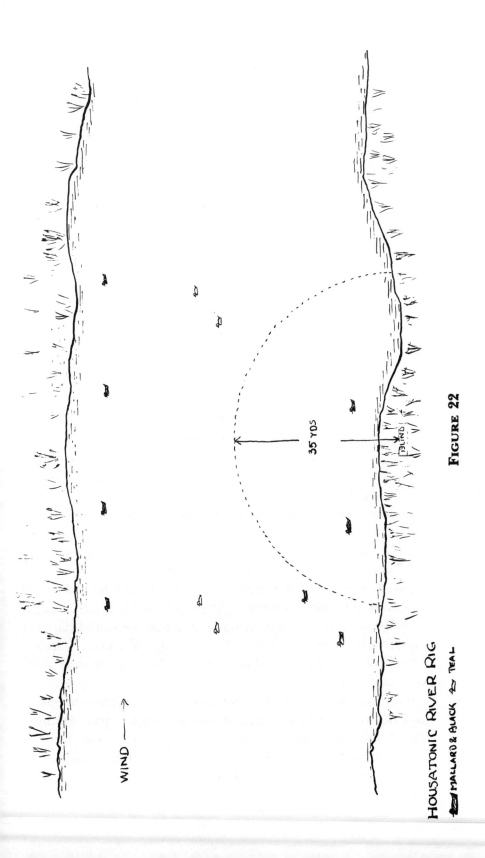

WIND ⟶

35 YDS

BLIND

HOUSATONIC RIVER RIG

MALLARD & BLACK & TEAL

FIGURE 22

no effort to solve the unknown. Sketched roughly, I will grant, and from memory—mine or someone else's—they show how one gunner rigged under the circumstances represented. I make no claim that these sets are perfect or that some other method might not have worked as well, but merely that these *did* work. I have tried to include enough rigging patterns so the reader may find one or several approximating his own situations and so get a hunch, a hint, about how to rig his decoys.

One of the baffling things about shooting with some of the old-timers was that just as I was convinced from watching them that I had learned some of their basic rules and could count on how they would solve a problem in rigging, they would put out a rig quite different from the one I expected. This probably proves there are many effective ways of handling a rigging problem. However, leaving such elaborations to those "who know a rule well enough to break it," here are a few *do's* and *don'ts* for a starting point.

Avoid the mistake of setting decoys too close together. When ducks are at rest on the water, they cover quite an area and are reasonably well separated. In the diagrams accompanying this chapter thirty-five-yard circles are drawn from the front of the blinds not so much to indicate range as to show the dispersion of decoys.

Figures 23 and 24 suggest the right and wrong ways to handle a dozen decoys in front of a shore blind. Note, in Figure 23, the open area in the decoy pattern to the right of the blind. Decoying birds will have their brakes set and be aiming for this spot. In Figure 24 the decoys are far out and bunched and ducks would probably try to light outside and behind them. At the first shot, if any were in range, the balance would flare off rapidly downwind and be promptly out of range. Careless handling of decoys, like this, makes for long going-away shots and cripples.

Group decoys by species, mallards together, pintails together, bluebill together, rather than mixing them up. If your gunning stand offers shooting at both diving ducks and surface feeders, separate the two varieties of decoys. Set them in relation to your

[76]

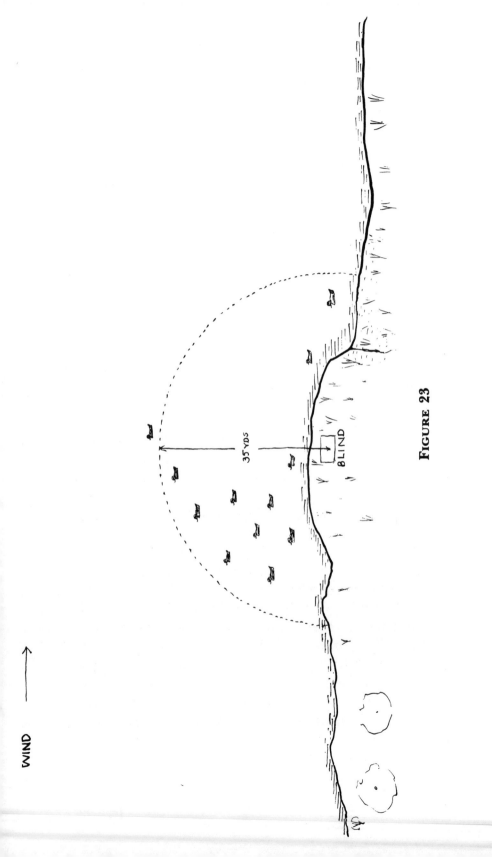

WIND →

35 YDS

BLIND

FIGURE 23

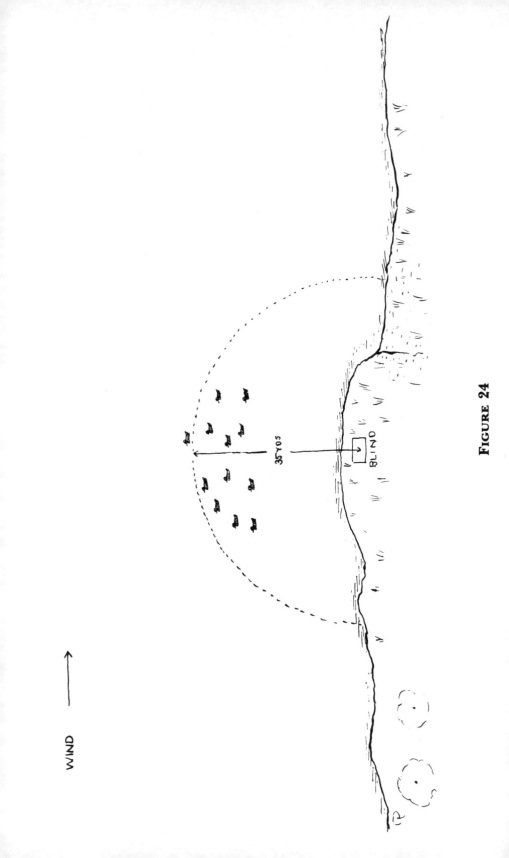

WIND ⟶

35 YDS

BLIND

FIGURE 24

blind on the theory that diving ducks will tend to light to the head of a rig and shoal-water ducks to light short of your decoys. While geese will cross over duck decoys, ducks do not like to cross goose decoys and shoal-water ducks do not like to fly over any decoys. These are generalities and at times ducks will behave in different ways than those indicated. "Green" ducks will come slamming into your decoys any old way and in a storm birds will decoy as they will not in better weather. These suggestions, like all others in this book, may be disregarded when your own experience recommends a different method, a better way of doing things in your area. However, these ideas, based on considerable composite experience, *should be* given a thorough trial.

There is a variety of opinion about including goose decoys in a duck rig. "Always add a few geese," says one school, while the other holds that goose decoys tend to scare ducks off. These seemingly contradictory opinions are both so firmly held that I am convinced each is based on sound experience. They appear to have a geographic pattern, so I suggest that local custom among competent gunners be followed. I have found a few geese decoys, if properly set, do not interfere with decoying ducks. Except for their size and great visibility they do not, by me, add to the effectiveness of a rig. If geese are not likely to be flying, I prefer oversize duck decoys as *tollers*. In an area where a shot at a goose is always a possibility, it is wise to have goose decoys. A few decoys plus a good goose call are worth a great deal on that occasion when the honkers unexpectedly appear.

One point about this goose-duck-decoy controversy seems firmly settled. I have seen experts pick up their duck decoys and leave only goose stool out when they felt, because of a change in the weather or some other factor, good goose shooting was probable. I conclude therefore that while geese will decoy to a mixed rig of duck and goose decoys, the evidence is they can be expected to decoy more readily to goose decoys alone.

There is no firm rule about the number of decoys to be used. Diving ducks are more gregarious and move in greater flights

[79]

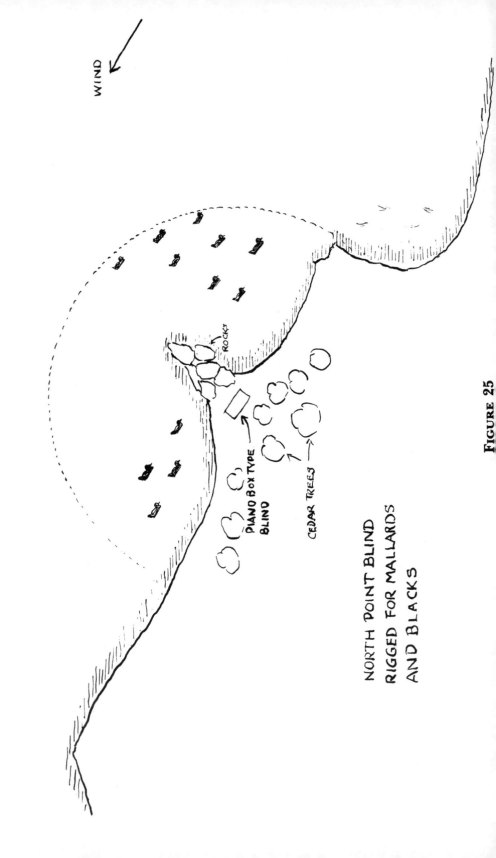

WIND

ROCKS

PIANO BOX TYPE
BLIND

CEDAR TREES →

NORTH POINT BLIND
RIGGED FOR MALLARDS
AND BLACKS

FIGURE 25

than shoal-water birds. For canvasback, redhead, bluebill, and so forth, much larger quantities of decoys are used than for mallards, blacks, widgeon, or pintail. I have frequently heard the expression, "Big water, big rig." I go along with it as a safe generality; but in shooting from shore blinds I believe there is definitely such a thing as too many decoys. I shoot from a blind on an exposed point of an island in a lake that is five miles east and west and has fifteen miles of open water north of this point.

That is big water by my definition, but a rig of a dozen blacks and mallards is all we use. Add a half-dozen pintail or widgeon when they are flying and, if your decoys are good, you have all you need. I will not say that a few more would be a disadvantage, but I do question whether they justify the time and effort involved in setting them out and picking them up. In a more protected spot on the same island six or eight decoys are plenty when we are gunning shoal-water birds. On another point running out into deep water we shoot bluebill and whistlers and for them we will put out six dozen decoys. There you have it. In three different locations on the same small island we rig anywhere from six to seventy decoys. The birds moving, wind direction, and the time of year are all factors in deciding on location and number as well as types of decoys to be used.

Rigs should have about the same number of hens and drakes, except for those species where there is little plumage difference between the sexes such as black duck, brant, and Canada geese. Some gunners err on the side of the more spectacular drakes in both buying and rigging, but a study of old decoys belonging to market hunters shows hens to be in the majority. Fifty-fifty is a good rule for the beginner until his own experience indicates a reason for changing.

I had my confidence in this point shaken recently when I discovered men who are "experts" in gunning for redhead and canvasback using a majority of drakes in their rigs. I hunted up an old market gunner who hunts now only for his own pleasure and asked him about it. "It's the gunners, not the ducks," he told me. "The 'cans' will still decoy better to a mixed rig. I have

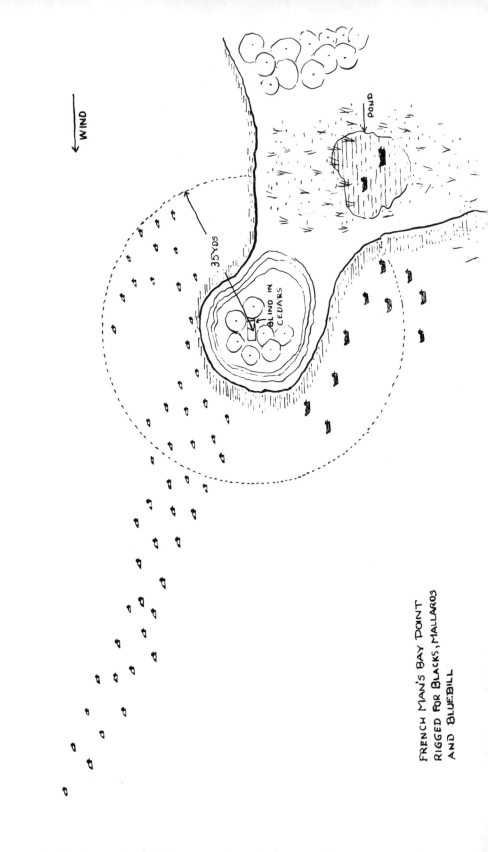

WIND

35 YDS

BLIND IN CEDARS

POND

FRENCH MAN'S BAY POINT
RIGGED FOR BLACKS, MALLARDS
AND BLUEBILL

several hundred decoys to choose from and plenty of drakes in the lot, but I still rig mostly hens."

There are several local factors which may affect this matter of the relation between hens and drakes. In some areas there are separate and distinct flights of hens and drakes and this can necessitate special rigging during these flights. Another seasonal and regional factor to be remembered is the developing plumage patterns in certain species. Decoys painted to represent late-season or full-plumage birds are out of place in a rig when early-season birds are still in molt. A drake mallard in full plumage with a dark green head and black upturned tail feathers will prove far from a lure if used too early. Shooting along the Canadian border at the very start of the season, for example, I use only hen mallards, as at this time of year hens and drakes are almost alike. Any gunner who expects more than casual success should become familiar with changing plumage patterns and adjust his use of decoys to coincide.

There is an easy way to learn about rigging a particular location, whether bay, point, or river: Watch from a distance through binoculars and see how ducks behave there. Preseason study of ducks will pay big dividends. If you cannot watch from a distance with glasses, watch at closer range, but keep completely hidden so that ducks will be absolutely unaware of your presence and hence behave naturally.

One excellent guide who used to rig part of his decoys onshore near his blind told me he learned the trick by watching ducks before the season. "Taught me a thing or two," he said. "Used to rig decoys as far out as fifty yards; now my farthest decoy isn't twenty yards from the blind. Found the ducks almost always ashore here and close into shore when they come in with no one in the blind. Get more birds in range than we used to."

His blind had to be good, of course, but any duck hunter who puts up with less than the best possible blind might better get up later in the morning and go pheasant shooting.

This preseason watching will also give some hint as to where to rig in relation to the blind. It will take actual shooting to settle this, but remember the purpose of decoys is to bring ducks well

[83]

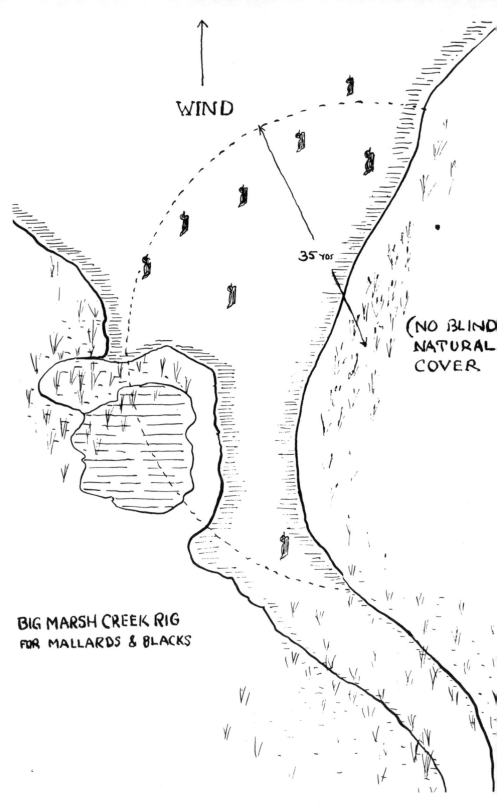

WIND

35 YDS

(NO BLIND
NATURAL
COVER

BIG MARSH CREEK RIG
FOR MALLARDS & BLACKS

FIGURE 27

within range; and the exact place to put decoys to serve this purpose is frequently not directly in front of your blind. Watch the ducks and if necessary move either the blind or the decoys, whichever is easier, so you bring the ducks before you. In heavy crosswinds I have had the decoys well out of range to one side or the other to bring the ducks into range.

Every gunner who keeps a shooting diary considers it a priceless possession, and those of us who do not keep one are aware that we are missing part of the pleasure we are entitled to derive from our sport. I bring the subject up here because it has a bearing on rigging decoys. The nearest I ever came to keeping such a record had to do with shooting in a new area with a group, all of us unfamiliar with local conditions. For several years a record was kept by those who shot and by the end of the third year it had become invaluable. This was no elaborate leather-covered ledger, but a notebook with mimeographed pages. We set up a typical page after a good bit of discussion as to what we wanted, and then had a couple of hundred run off on a mimeograph machine. Total cost, including a ringed binder, was four dollars and seventy-five cents.

A practical proof of the value of the shooting record turned up on a bluebird day. I had three guests at the island. On our first day we had some shooting on a northwest wind in the morning. Both the wind and the shooting faded out about noon and never came back. Driving in from the dock at dusk to the little country hotel that served us as "camp," we turned on the car radio and heard the dismal weather forecast for the next day: "Fair and warmer with light southwest winds diminishing in the forenoon."

After dinner it was my duty to "post the books." My companions asked about our record—how and why we kept them. One of them said, "Well, see what your records say we should do on a damned bluebird day like the one coming up tomorrow."

We found a number of bluebird days recorded, none of them very promising, but of all the places that had been rigged, one was clearly the best choice on calm days. Without a study of "the book" its choice would never have occurred to me. The diagram

[85]

PAGE FROM THE SHOOTING DIARY

Date_____

Temperature at start of day_____at end of day_____

Barometer at start of day_____at end of day_____

Wind direction_____estimated force_____miles per hour.

Changes in wind during day. What_____when_____

Remarks about wind_____

Weather.
Rain_____Snow_____Fair_____Overcast_____

Remarks about weather_____

Blinds used & number of people in each location.

_____ _____ _____ _____

Names of people shooting._____

_____

_____

Ducks killed

Number_____Species_____Blind_____

Number_____Species_____Blind_____

Number_____Species_____Blind_____

Decoys used—number and type at each blind.

_____ _____ _____ _____

Ducks in range (estimated)_____Species_____

Ducks seen not in range (estimated)_____Species_____

Time of first shot_____Time of last shot_____

Time of best shooting. From_____to_____

Comments and suggestions._____

_____

_____

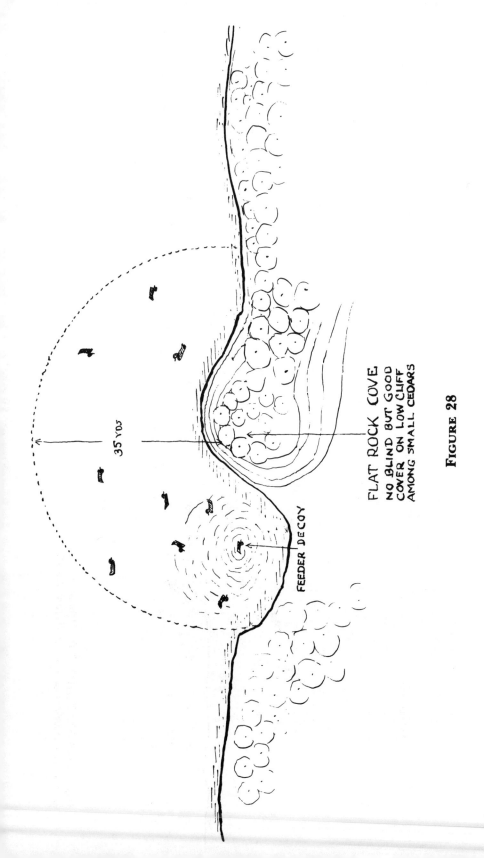

35 YDS

FEEDER DECOY

FLAT ROCK COVE
NO BLIND BUT GOOD
COVER ON LOW CLIFF
AMONG SMALL CEDARS

FIGURE 28

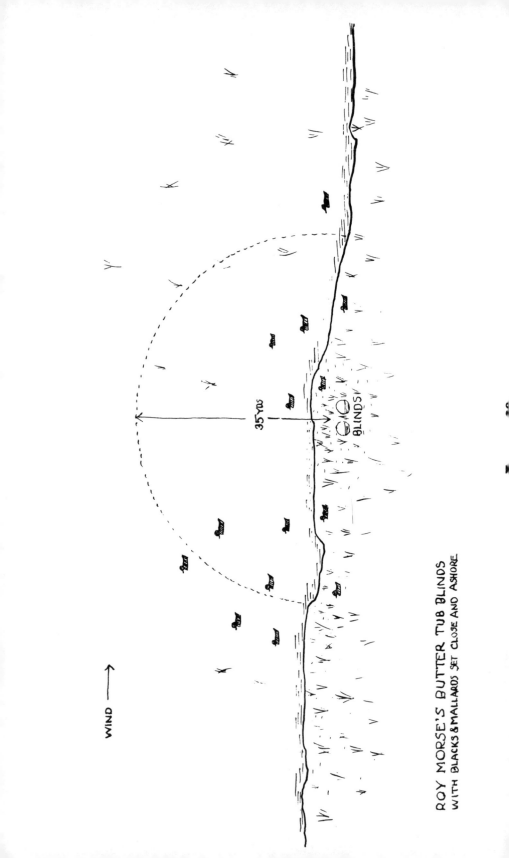

ROY MORSE'S BUTTER TUB BLINDS
WITH BLACKS & MALLARDS SET CLOSE AND ASHORE

of Flat Rock Cove (see Figure 28) shows how we rigged. Our outer decoys might have been set on mirrors as far as motion went, but they were visible at great distances and we kept a feeder decoy working to produce action on the water close to shore. We used a duck call whenever birds were in sight, and managed to get some shooting.

At the start we religiously posted the book each night when we got in. Of the first thirty-seven days recorded, I was present only eleven, but because of our record-keeping my knowledge of local duck behavior under varying conditions was more than three times as great as it could have been based on personal experience alone.

Have we kept it up? Certainly not! We are much too smart for that. We learned everything there was to know after a few years. Finally somebody lost the record book. Fortunately, some of what we had written down and studied many times stayed in our heads, but not enough, I am sure, to offset the advantages the records would have given us.

You remember the story of the man who was ordered by his doctor to stop drinking. A few days later he saw this same doctor having a few with the boys at the club bar, and took him to task.

"You pay me for advice," the doctor explained. "Follow my advice, not my example."

Well, take my advice. To learn about duck shooting and rigging decoys keep a record. And keep on keeping it.

11.

Rigging Offshore Blinds

The same basic principles of rigging apply wherever you set decoys—from shore blinds or offshore blinds, for shoal-water duck will tend to light short of the decoys and divers will light into the rig or ahead of it. The chief difference is that with water on all sides you have twice as much area for decoys around an offshore blind. The lack of shoreline makes it easier to rig. It is simpler, for example, to keep the species separate and allow duck to come to your decoys naturally, but it also gives approaching duck more latitude and your decoys must be set to lead them into range. The pipe-stem, fish-hook, or big-dipper set requires a large number of decoys, but generally pays dividends with the divers.

If your blind is in deep water and you are gunning primarily for diving ducks, it is often profitable to rig shoal-water decoys, mallards, blacks, or pintails, unless none are using in the area or experience proves they will not decoy. It certainly is not uncommon to see shoal-water ducks lying near canvasback or redhead.

Many things, including the law, will affect your location. You are fortunate if you can locate your blind on a channel or where shallow water drops off into deep water—"along an edge" the old-timers called it. Diving duck will frequently follow such

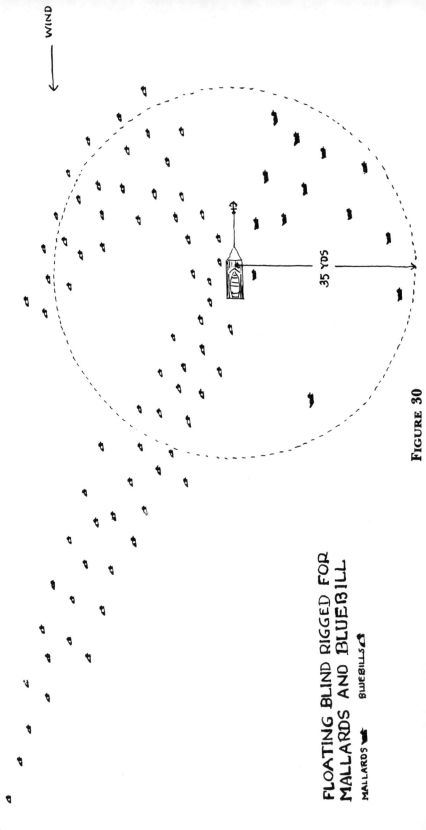

WIND

35 YDS

FLOATING BLIND RIGGED FOR
MALLARDS AND BLUEBILL

MALLARDS   BLUEBILLS

FIGURE 30

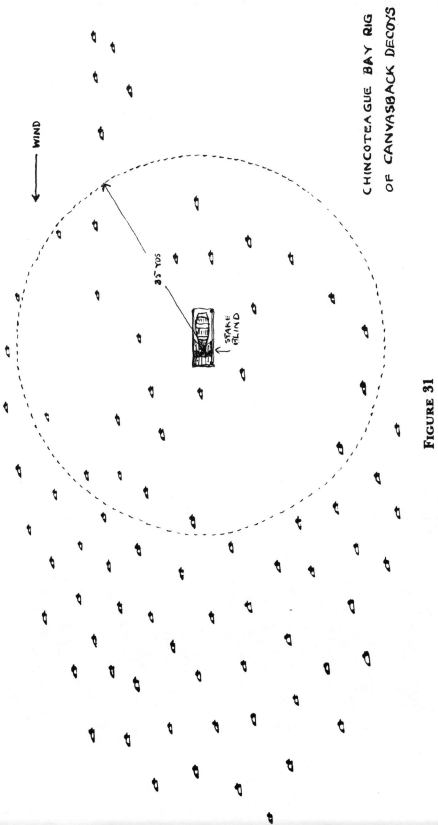

CHINCOTEAGUE BAY RIG
OF CANVASBACK DECOYS

WIND

35 YDS

STAKE
BLIND

FIGURE 31

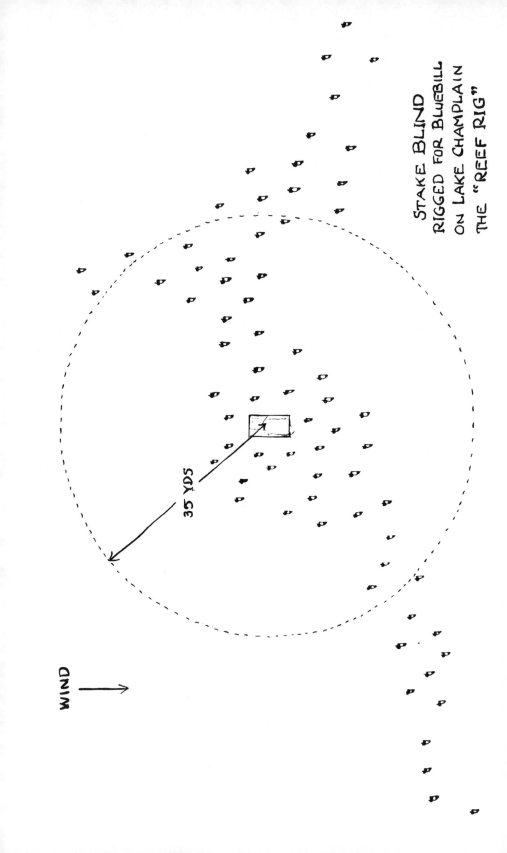

WIND →

35 YDS

STAKE BLIND
RIGGED FOR BLUEBILL
ON LAKE CHAMPLAIN
THE "REEF RIG"

defined courses and this enables you to rig in a natural line of flight. It is obvious that your blind is best set where there is natural food.

Depth of water, wind direction, closeness of shorelines, and normal flight paths are all elements to be taken into consideration when you decide how to place decoys. If you are undecided, try rigging your divers on the side farthest from shore.

Floating blinds and stake blinds are rigged alike and each has advantages and disadvantages. A floating blind can be towed to a new location if conditions change, but this is not necessarily helpful unless you have fresh flight birds arriving. Resident ducks will probably give it a wide berth for a time after it is relocated. In heavy weather, in an exposed location, a stake blind has the great advantage of providing a stable shooting platform. There is something disconcerting in having the roll of a floating blind added to the customary difficulties of hitting ducks which are flaring off downwind in a blow.

Figure 30 shows a good rig for either a floating or stake blind. Shoal-water ducks are rigged to one side of the blind and a long line of diver decoys lead into a typical big-dipper set. The thirty-five yard circle around the blind is intended to indicate the placing of decoys rather than to mark range.

Figure 31 shows a canvasback set used by a most skillful guide around his stake blind in Chincoteague Bay, Virginia. Incidentally, this blind was built high enough to house a boat underneath it, and while it stood out like a lighthouse, the canvasback apparently accepted it as "belonging," for they decoyed beautifully to this rig.

Figure 32 shows an unusual rig developed by a shrewd Vermont guide on Lake Champlain for late-season bluebill shooting. He called it a "reef set" and explained that bluebill strung out in such a thin, wavy line when they were feeding over a shoal. The duck approved, evidently, for we had fine shooting there.

12.

Sneak-shooting Rigs

The first sneak boat was probably a dugout or a birch-bark canoe on which an Indian piled branches to hide behind. With arrow notched and strung, he drifted downwind on canvasback rafted over wild celery beds. We may speculate that this foxy early American soon figured that decoys would help hold his birds. We *know* he was using canvasback decoys a thousand or so years ago, and since he preferred stationary targets, it seems safe to presume he was the originator of the business of setting decoys, watching them from a distance until duck lit in with them and then paddling or drifting down to shoot. Do not think the Indian could not kill duck on the wing with bow and arrow. He could and did. I have a friend on the Pacific coast today who kills duck this way. He refuses to tell how many arrows he uses to kill a duck, but insists the Indian must have had a fairly good ratio, for he could shoot better and his birds were not so wary.

Sneak shooting has developed along diverse lines in different parts of the country, and boats have been produced for this type of hunting peculiar to the localities. A variant of sneak shooting that most closely follows the aboriginal method is practiced on the upper Hudson River in New York State where the boat normally used is a narrow, lightweight rowboat of the kind used in the Adirondack Mountains and there carried on portages

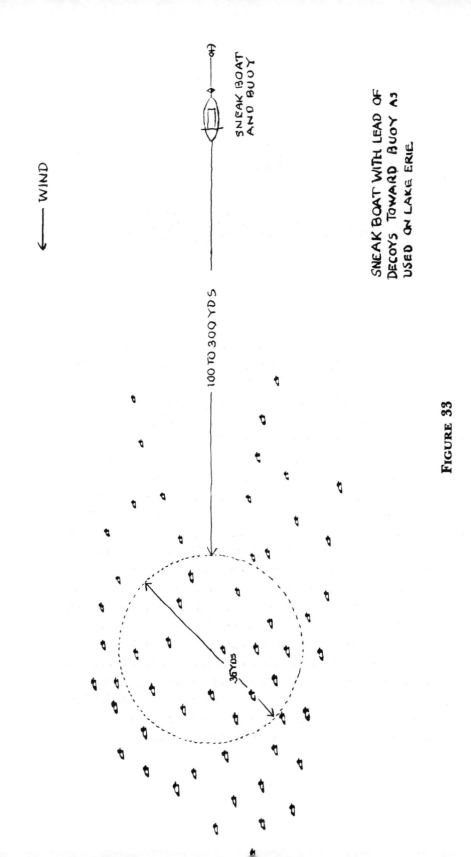

WIND

SNEAK BOAT
AND BUOY

100 TO 300 YDS

36 YDS

SNEAK BOAT WITH LEAD OF
DECOYS TOWARD BUOY AS
USED ON LAKE ERIE

FIGURE 33

like a canoe and called a *guide boat*. The screen for sneak shooting is made by drilling holes in a piece of board, roughly two by six inches and long enough to extend about a foot beyond each side of the boat; cedar branches are fitted into the holes so they stand two feet above the gunwales of the boat when the board is laid across them forward of the gunner. A double row of holes in the ends that extend overside allow some cedars to be inserted from the underside so they drag in the water, helping to conceal the paddles. The gunner and the paddler sit on the bottom of the boat, thus reducing visibility and increasing stability. The paddler uses short-handled paddles not unlike Ping-pong rackets and has remarkable control over his slim craft.

The boats used on the Housatonic and Connecticut rivers and in Long Island Sound have relatively little in common with either the Merrymeeting Bay boat of the Maine coast or those of the Mississippi Basin. The various boats were ideal for their special situations and many local builders acquired outstanding reputations for their craft. They would spend days in those more leisurely times looking through lumber yards to find just exactly the white pine or cedar they wanted for a new hull. A sneak boat was proudly identified by the name of its builder, or an owner would explain of a new boat that he "took the lines off an *Alfred* or a *MacMillan*." More sneak shooting is done today on the Great Lakes and on the rivers and bays adjoining them than elsewhere. Boats, rigs, and decoys have been brought to a high stage of perfection on Lake St. Clair, the Detroit River, and western Lake Erie and are illustrated.

The usual method of handling a boat after decoys have been set—in a great oval if in open water—is to anchor a buoy upwind from the rig and to lie to this buoy until duck have lit in the decoys. The line from the buoy is cast off and the sneak boat is paddled or steered, depending somewhat on the strength of the breeze, and moves down on the decoys. The plywood screen acts as a sail and, if the wind is strong, aids in the necessarily fast trip, for duck will not stay indefinitely, even with the best of

[99]

decoys. Good guides and good gunners really dig in with their paddles to hurry into shooting range. There is no set rule as to how far away from the decoys the buoy should be set. Far enough not to spook the ducks, obviously, but not any farther than is necessary, for the downwind trip must be made quickly and the upwind trip after picking up the kill can be arduous against the seas. Sometimes the buoy is set as much as three hundred yards away, two hundred to two-fifty is more nearly average; and in rain, fog, or snow with birds piling in you may occasionally lie just outside your decoys.

In the two-man sneak boat of the Great Lakes the man in the bow is the gunner. He watches the ducks through holes cut in the screen that is held in place across the boat in front of him. He directs the paddler with hand signals and also paddles if the need for speed requires that he do so. When he is in range he drops the screen and shoots. The stern man does not shoot unless there is complete teamwork between the two and they have great confidence in each other. The danger is apparent. Two brothers I know have shot together from the same boat for over fifty years. At a signal the stern man gives his paddle a prodigious flip and swings the sneak boat broadside to the wind, giving each man a fair, safe shot at the rising ducks. Taking turn and turnabout at the two positions is the more usual procedure, with only the bow man shooting. One guide of my acquaintance does all the paddling and kneels jammed against the back of his "sport," thus reassuring him that he is in no position to handle a gun. It also makes the guide sure that the customer cannot swing around and pot him.

While hand signals are used to direct the steerer, low voices do not seem to bother the ducks, but a bump with a paddle against the side of the boat will send them into the air. Care should be taken in rigging to leave an open path into the decoys where the boat can enter the rig with no danger of banging a decoy, for this will spook duck as quickly as a bump with a paddle.

[100]

Sneak shooting as we know it today was largely developed by the market hunters. Canvasback have always been considered the most desirable duck for the table, and their tendency to feed in open water far from the shore blinds sent the market gunner looking for methods of offshore pursuit—hence the battery, the layout boat, and the sneak rig. Even before the turn of the century, when shooting for the market still had twenty years to go, a pair of "cans" would sometimes bring five dollars. The men who could kill a hundred pair a day could afford to perfect their rigs—and did. The price of a good sneak boat, even an old one in good repair, will shock the inexperienced.

Sneak shooting is for the experts. There is no tougher test for decoys or rigging. The rig must be good enough to bring the duck in, lighting holes must be provided so the duck will light into the part of the rig where you want them when you come into range, and the decoys must be excellent to persuade the ducks sitting among them to stay when the sneak boat is coming down on them. In most circumstances the rig is on big open water and if there is wind to move ducks around there is plenty to kick up a sea so the gunner has the added hazard of shooting from a small boat that is rolling and pitching. Boat handling of the finest sort is required. Big rigs of decoys are necessary and they often have to be shifted several times during a day, for any change in the direction of the wind will affect the course the boat follows on the sneak and the way the ducks jump when they get out of the decoys.

Hy Dahlka of Gibraltar, Michigan, explains it this way: "You must come directly downwind to make a good sneak and have your ducks get out as you want them to do. The trick is to lie at your buoy with the wind hitting you squarely on both ears. If you begin to feel the wind stronger on one ear than the other it's time to move your buoy or your rig or both."

Before they have been under gunning pressure, early in the season, or in extreme weather, blacks and mallards will sometimes decoy to a rig of divers. They are not above stealing food

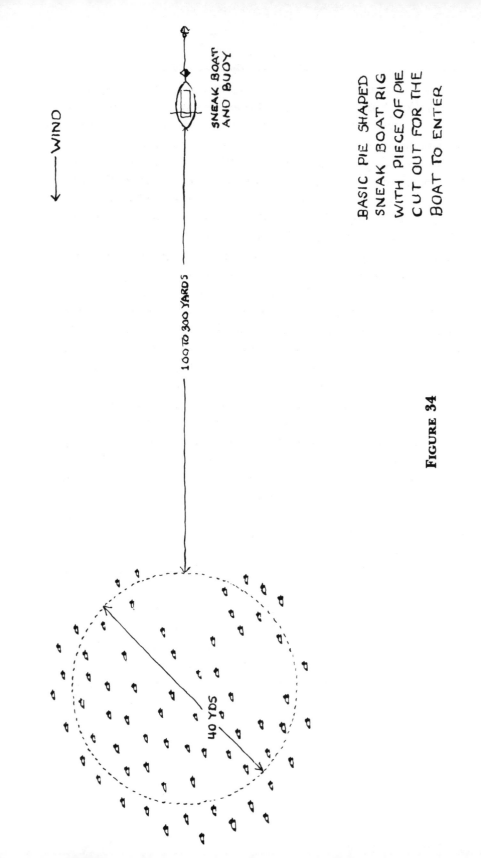

WIND

100 TO 300 YARDS

40 YDS

SNEAK BOAT
AND BUOY

BASIC PIE SHAPED
SNEAK BOAT RIG
WITH PIECE OF PIE
CUT OUT FOR THE
BOAT TO ENTER

FIGURE 34

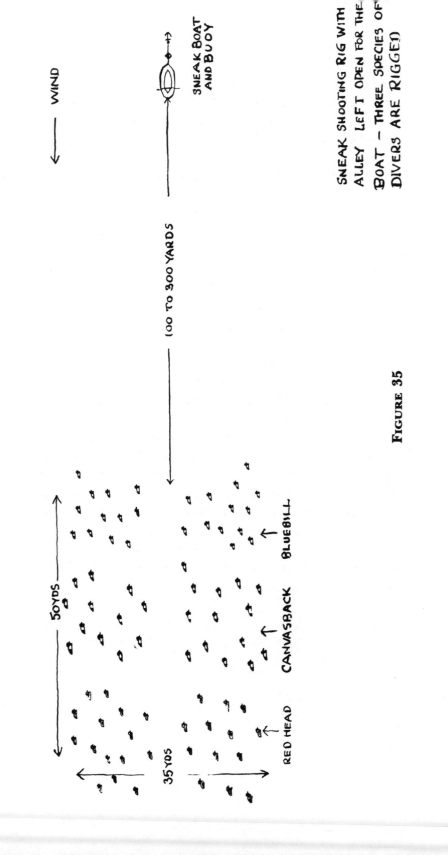

WIND

SNEAK BOAT AND BUOY

100 TO 300 YARDS

50 YDS

35 YDS

RED HEAD   CANVASBACK   BLUEBILL

SNEAK SHOOTING RIG WITH ALLEY LEFT OPEN FOR THE BOAT — THREE SPECIES OF DIVERS ARE RIGGED

FIGURE 35

the divers have hauled up from below. They will not hold in the decoys, however, and the birds usually rigged and gunned for with sneak rigs are canvasback, redhead, and bluebill. In setting a rig of decoys the bluebill are placed upwind at the head of the rig and nearest the sneak boat at its buoy. The canvasback are placed in the middle and the redhead downwind at the tail of the rig. This is done because this is the order in which the duck will spook. Bluebill lighting in the rig will be the first to swim away or take off before the sneak can be completed, thus they are placed to bring them into range most quickly. The redhead, notably a dumb duck, will hold even after the bluebill and canvasback have been alerted and taken wing. A friend who does a good deal of sneak shooting writes me that he has killed canvasback and had time to reload and move on down through the rig and get a shot at redhead still hanging around.

Many guides do not rig for bluebill, hoping to provide their customers with the more delectable canvasback and because the scary bluebill getting out will sometimes spook canvasback, if both are in the decoys, before the sneak boat is in range. The size of a rig for sneak shooting depends on weather conditions, the amount of competition, the size of the body of water, and many other factors. The experts refer to a rig of seventy-five or eighty decoys as "small" and rigs of several hundred are not uncommon. One guide describing his manner of rigging told me, "Leave plenty of lighting holes and keep your decoys well separated—at least four feet of water between decoys. Get somebody to fly you over where 'cans' are rafted an' see. They don't set so snug."

13.

Layout Boats and Rigs

Like the almost-forgotten battery, for which it is in some measure a substitute, the layout boat is basically a one-man outfit. Two-man boats are sometimes built, but the mere increase in size tends to defeat the purpose for which they are designed: to be nearly invisible when anchored in the middle of a large spread of decoys. Normal procedure calls for a tender, usually a power boat, from which the rig is set and the kill picked up. Gunners take turns shooting from the layout boat, sometimes changing places on an hourly basis, after a certain number of shots, or according to some other prearranged plan.

The grass boat, often a layout boat with grass added to the decks and along the rails as camouflage, is used in much the same way—the chief difference being that the grass boat is customarily used in a marsh area, possibly shoved into the edge of the marsh to act as a low blind partly hidden and blending with its surroundings. There is no firm rule about it, of course, but the grass boat is more likely to be used for shoal-water ducks, whereas the true layout boat is generally used for divers on open water and has no camouflage, relying for concealment on its low freeboard and on being painted in the closest possible match to the color of the water where it is anchored.

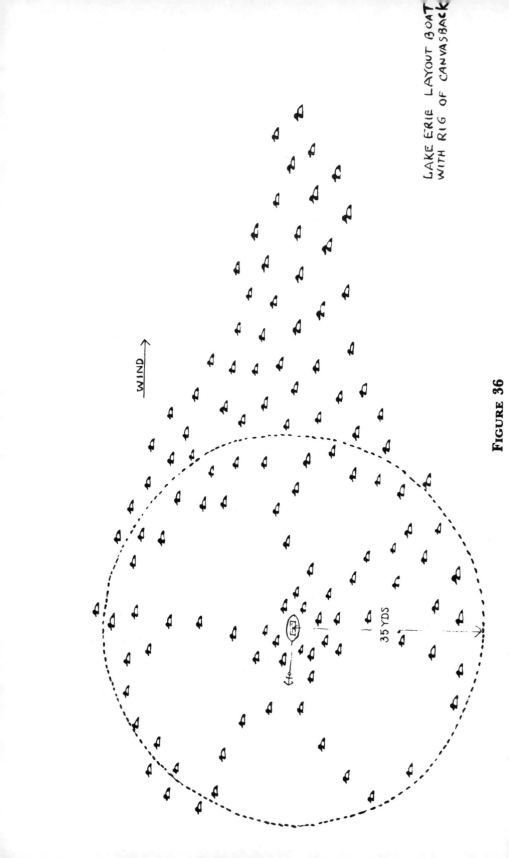

WIND →

35 YDS

LAKE ERIE LAYOUT BOAT
WITH RIG OF CANVASBACK

FIGURE 36

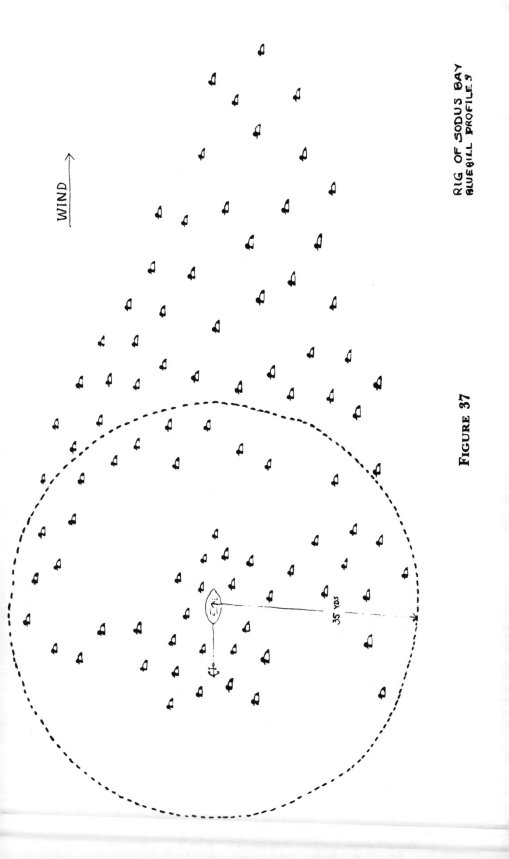

WIND →

35 YDS

RIG OF SODUS BAY
BLUEBILL PROFILE 3

FIGURE 37

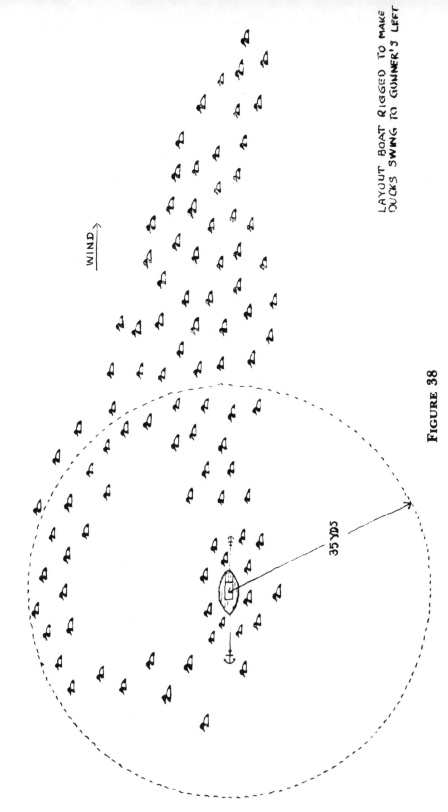

WIND →

35 YDS

LAYOUT BOAT RIGGED TO MAKE
DUCKS SWING TO GUNNER'S LEFT

FIGURE 38

With the grass boat in shoal water much the same rig of decoys is used as would be used with a shore blind in the same area. The layout boat in exposed water calls for a larger rig of decoys, some of which are set close to the boat in an effort to break up its outlines and make it less visible. Essentially the term *layout boat* applies to a variety of regional boats usually small, low-lying, and with narrow cockpits in which the gunner lies protected from the seas by wide decks and high coamings. The Long Island scooter, the Connecticut scull boat, the Great Lakes layout boat, the Barnegat Bay sneak box, the grass boat of the northern lakes, and the camouflaged pirogue of Louisiana all serve the same purpose. In fact, each fits its particular habitat but would not do as well in another environment.

Certainly the duck hunter interested in acquiring a layout boat ought to study those in local use and either buy a boat that has already proved itself, or have a local and experienced builder who has successful boats to his credit build one to order. The wrong boat will not prove very useful and may even be dangerous.

Layout boats are anchored bow to wind and sea, with the gunner lying with his head upwind so he sees the ducks coming into his decoys. If there is a heavy sea or if wind and current tend to make the boat yaw or lie crosswind, a stern anchor is set. The rigs shown in Figures 36 and 37 are somewhat similar, both having open areas in the spread of decoys called lighting holes. With diving ducks these tend to pull ducks down if they are coming high, although they may still aim for the head of the rig before lighting.

Skillful guides used to rig decoys around a battery to swing ducks right or left, depending on which way the gunner preferred to shoot. This practice is sometimes followed with layout boat rigs and Figure 38 shows a left-hand rig.

Drakes and hens are mixed up in a rig, but different species are kept more or less separate—canvasback together, redhead together, etc.

[111]

If both divers and shoal-water ducks are likely to be flying and decoys for both are to be set around a layout boat, remember to keep the two types well separated. Figure 30 in Chapter 11 will suggest a type of rig to be used where the shoal-water ducks are given an opportunity to light short of the decoys, and the divers may be expected to cross or come well into the deep-water decoys.

14.

Care, Painting, and
Storage of Decoys

Decoys get rugged use and the best of them need care. When the thermometer stands below freezing and ice forms on anchor lines, no duck hunter can be blamed for hurriedly tumbling decoys in his boat, but he should remember that this sort of treatment and other rough handling cause damage which must be repaired. During the season some decoys get broken bills, banged-up heads, or have their paint badly marred, and are usually put aside for later overhaul.

One hunter of my acquaintance takes his entire rig to a local decoy-maker when he is through with it for the year and pays to have repairs, painting, or rerigging done. This is fine for him, but tinkering with decoys makes good wintertime fun for most of us.

At the end of the gunning year I take the anchor lines off my decoys and plan to replace them unless careful testing shows they are good for another season. Getting out a boat and chasing drifting decoys is not a favorite occupation of mine, and to avoid it I check lines, anchors, staples, swivels, and all parts of the ground tackle each year. Some of the decoys may be so badly beaten up that they need to be replaced or you may want to add to your rig—the end of the season is the time to do it. You can wait for delivery for just what you want whether you order by mail, from your sporting-goods dealer, or have decoys turned out by a local *jackknife sculptor.*

I begin the season-end care by scrubbing my decoys with a stiff brush and mild soap and water. Do not use detergents or too strong a soap that will take the paint off. Decoys get dirty or stained and any weathered paint will scrub off, disclosing a need for repainting that might not otherwise appear until they were put in service again. Decoys are best stored in a cellar, woodshed, or wherever they will not be subjected to extreme dry heat. String decoys together in two's and three's and hang them from spikes rather than leave them on the floor where they may be kicked around.

After the decoys have been scrubbed, rinsed, and are thoroughly dry, they should be checked for loose heads, keels, or weights. If heads or keels are loose they should be removed and replaced, although sometimes drilling additional holes and redowling will work. When you use dowls, set them in reliable marine or waterproof glue. Dents and shot holes in wooden decoys can be filled with plastic wood, sanded, and repainted. Shot holes in plastic decoys can be repaired with material available from their makers.

Repainting a few decoys which are part of a rig requires careful planning in order to avoid contrast between those that are freshly painted and the duller appearance of decoys that have weathered through a season or two. Old-time makers painted decoys and exposed them to rain and sun. Charles DoVille of Sodus Bay used to hang newly painted decoys from the outer eaves of his workshop to "tone 'em down." If most of a rig needs painting it is wise to repaint the entire lot to avoid contrast.

The decoys set aside for repainting can be lightly sanded. Many times there will be paint enough left on the decoys so the pattern can be followed in painting. Some gunners make a rough sketch of patterns and colors; others lightly carve outlines to show the division of colors. I long ago gave up buying house paint and trying to mix my own decoy colors. Paints for

[116]

decoys must not shine and the colors should be *just right.* I buy paint made for decoys but sometimes blend the colors.

When you are repainting decoys, paint the undersides in a rough approximation at the top. A drake bluebill, for instance, with the bottom painted a light gray with black ends, is far less conspicuous floating wrong side up than it would be in any solid color, particularly white.

When you are through painting, inspect your decoys carefully and if you find them shiny, try rubbing them lightly with powdered pumice or resort to the old makers' trick and leave them out in the weather for a few weeks. A few shiny or badly painted decoys can ruin an entire rig.

Careful transportation and storage can add measurably to the life of decoys and reduce the need for repainting and repairs. In fact, most damage to decoys occurs while they are being transported rather than when in use. What you can do to protect them and lessen this hazard will depend on the type of decoy you use, where and how you store them during the season (and after), and many other factors. If you shoot from a boat or a location reached by boat, the ideal thing is to be able to leave your decoys aboard. Some Barnegat Bay boats and some of the scooters used along the New England coast have hatches that can be locked in place, thus providing safe storage. Some blinds, too, can be locked and so provide housing for decoys and other shooting gear. A lucky few can leave their decoys on the points or in the marshes where they shoot, but most of us have to carry our decoys all or part of the way to our shooting stands and this calls for some method of protecting them in transit.

Charles Disbrow used the double-handled canvas sacks made for coal delivery. They held six decoys each, gave a measure of protection when stored in his car, and were not too heavy or unhandy when swung up on the shoulder as coalmen carried them. A South Carolina gunner has a container not unlike the canvas firewood-carriers made with leather handles that are in general use. This is made with pockets, four to a side, into

[117]

which decoys fit. The carrier is fitted with shoulder straps and one man can "tote it quite a piece," as they say down there. Anchors and lines are carried separately in another small canvas sack.

However you work it out, it is best to keep your decoys in small groups so they can be carried easily and protected from too much banging around. From time to time devices have come on the market for storing anchor lines on spring rollers fastened to the bottom of the decoys or contained in a hollowed-out cavity in the bottom. So far I have not found one that would stand the rigorous service required. The idea is fine, but the mechanisms have proved too complicated or too delicate. Line wound round the decoy and kept from unwinding by having an anchor that will slip over the decoy's head is a time-tested scheme for handling deep-water decoys where long lines are used. This makes for speed in setting out and picking up, but I prefer detaching anchor lines and storing them separately wound round the anchors. There is less chance of damaging the decoy this way.

If you use a boat, get your decoys organized before you leave the shore. Be sure you can handle them in the dark and the cold and perhaps while your boat is getting a thorough tossing-around in a sea.

15.

Duck and Goose Calls

My introduction to duck calling occurred in the Mayflower Hotel in Washington, D.C., when I was attending a North American Wildlife Conference. I was spending an evening with a redoubtable group of gunners, including such stalwarts as Charles Hopkins, Nash Buckingham, and the late Colonel H.P. Sheldon. It was to be expected that, considering the occasion and the company, in a long evening the talk would turn to duck shooting, the decreasing supply of birds, and the growing problems facing the gunner. In the course of the conversation Nash Buckingham, an outstanding shot and a keen student of every phase of wildfowling, made a statement about attracting ducks that I would have discounted had it come from a lesser authority. There were many sections of the country, he said, where if he had to choose between decoys and a call he would choose the call. The ideal, he continued, was to use both.

There was such general agreement with him among these knowledgeable shooters that I realized here was a part of duck hunting of which I knew little or nothing. Except for occasional expeditions farther afield, my shooting had been confined to that part of the United States which lies east of Lake Michigan and north of the Virginia Capes—the northeast. This is the region where we knew least about calls and their proper use.

Once in a while I had shot with someone who did some calling "by mouth," but rarely with anyone who used a call—tentatively and rather badly. I did not believe in calls. More accurately, I had never given them a thought. After that evening, however, I resolved to learn something about them.

Before the opening of the next season I acquired several calls, listened to phonograph records, read several instruction books, and spent some preseason time trying to talk to ducks. I learned about as much as I know today about calling—which is not much. I am still far from expert and certainly have no suggestions to offer those fortunate enough to have grown up in a section of the country, like Reelfoot Lake in Tennessee, where calls and calling are understood. This chapter is for gunners who have known little about calls or how to use them.

Inexpert as I am, I have brought duck over my decoys and had shots I would not have had without calling. I must admit that I have probably chased away some potential shots; but recognizing my lack of ability as a caller, I now belong to the school of "don't call unless you think duck are going to pass you by and don't call after you have attracted their attention."

This is undoubtedly a lazy solution. It would be far better and provide better shooting to put in the time and practice necessary to become a real expert. My point is that anyone with eight or ten dollars to spend for calls, phonograph record, and instruction book can soon learn enough to help increase their bag. To become a true expert requires time and work, but once you have heard a "master" work a call, you will know what can be done. However, even the masters do not overdo it.

A Black guide with whom I once shot in the south was an expert caller, but for all his proficiency he used his call sparingly. "Cap'n, Ah believes in moderation," he said. "Yassuh! Ah believes in moderation 'special in eatin' turnips an' blowin' on a duck call. Ah kin git along on mou'ty little of bofe."

I asked this sportsman how he learned to call so well and his reply is the best advice I have ever heard on the subject. "Cap'n," he said, "they ain't but one way to learn duck talk an' that's to sit out thar in the ma'sh an' listen to ducks talk an' you talk back till even them duck think you soun' jes like a duck talkin'."

Three types of duck calls are frequently used. The best-known produces the familiar *quack* of the mallard and when tuned a little higher is also used for black duck. The experts use the same call for teal. Calls to reproduce the plaintive whistle of pintail and widgeon are inexpensive and relatively easy to use. The diving duck will not respond to any but their own calls, which are a reedy *burr-burr-burr*, varying in pitch with the different species. Calls are made for this burring sound, although some gunners imitate it fairly well on a mallard call. A good phonograph record of calling is well worth its cost if it only enables the gunner to identify these various calls. A wrong call, a mallard call to canvasback for instance, is more likely to flare them off than to bring them in.

Goose calling is another matter. It is much easier to learn to use a goose call, and geese, in my experience, respond more readily to calling. Half an hour with a goose call and a phonograph record or even an instruction booklet and you're in business. Goose decoys are desirable, of course, but I have repeatedly seen geese called into range over duck decoys.

An unusual demonstration of this occurred the last year that live decoys were allowed. I was a guest at a famous club on eastern Long Island. It was at the end of the season and goose shooting should have been at its best. We had several days of good duck shooting but had seen no geese. At breakfast on our last day the head guide announced we were in for a hard southwest blow, an ideal goose wind for an island blind. It was decided to concentrate all the live-goose decoys at this preferred location, leaving the other blinds with duck decoys only. The club rules called for drawing for blinds each day at breakfast, and my host was visibly disappointed when he failed to draw the desired goose location for us.

Half the guide's predictions came true. By the time we got across the bay and into the blinds, there was a near-gale from the southwest and almost as soon as it was light enough to shoot, we saw a big flock of geese beating their way slowly up the bay against the wind. The live decoys sent up welcoming *Ah-honks* from the island and my host began to call—pointlessly, I thought. He kept at it, however, and presently the flock wavered a bit in our direction and finally turned away from the blandishments of the real geese at the island and came to look us over, talking steadily. The wise old gander in the lead evidently missed seeing goose decoys or mistrusted something about our rig and turned the flock downwind away from us, but four tag-end geese in the flock were satisfied with my friend's calling and came sailing into range.

There was a good deal of wailing and gnashing of teeth in the other blind, for this proved to be the only goose flight of the day. One occupant of the island blind that day still insists this was just an early evidence of the "smooth talking" that led to my host's recent election to the governorship of his state. The governor and his state shall be nameless here to save any possible embarrassment. Great affairs press upon him now and he is not available these days for goose calling, but I have learned to do fairly well with a call. And so can you.

16.

General Hints on Equipment

Successful duck hunting requires great attention to detail. In shooting over decoys the plan is to entice ducks into range, and every care must be exercised to be sure no part of your own equipment defeats your purpose. One element off-color or out of place can ruin your shooting. The finest decoys properly set and a blind that is perfection can be purposeless if, for example, the top of your thermos bottle is exposed and reflects light because it has not been painted a dull, drab color or if you have forgotten to cover your outboard motor. Study every part of your equipment before the season starts with a view to painting, staining, or replacing anything that is too conspicuous.

Camouflage should have a more prominent part in a duck hunter's planning than it usually does. He should be more conscious of color in every part of his outfit when he buys it and when he uses it. According to Mr. Webster, camouflage is "to conceal by masking." Note the word is *masking*, not *hiding*. It is generally impossible to hide a duck boat used to tend a blind; but if the boat's color is right in the first place, the job of masking is made easier. Most gunners are aware of this and few turn up with a white or a bright red boat, but are not so thoughtful about other details of their outfit.

Shooting clothes should be selected in a color best calculated to blend with the shooting background. A warm brown may be perfect for a marsh blind and bad on a slate gray rocky point. If you move from your accustomed location, consider the possible need for some adjustment in the color of your clothing or equipment to fit the new surroundings. A friend, equipped for shooting in the marshes along the upper Hudson River, came up to shoot with me in northern Vermont on Lake Champlain. After we were rigged out on a cedar point, I took the boat down the lake a few miles to check another blind on which we had some work done. Coming back up the lake and upwind to join my companion, I discovered that his brown shooting coat, although partly hidden, still stood out against the background of cedars like a stop sign. In the case of ducks like a *"No Stop"* sign. We had an old, dirty piece of more or less colorless canvas to cover the outboard motor. We made a poncho of this by cutting a slit in the middle and he pulled it on over his head. It would have been better with a little green paint smeared on it, but it was far less conspicuous than his brown coat. We added a few cedar sprigs to his hat band and while he looked a bit ridiculous, he was certainly less visible. We felt a little sheepish. We both claim to be experienced duck hunters, but had I not gone down the lake we might have spent the day wondering why the ducks were passing us by.

Whether you make a poncho, sew grass on your hat, or smear mud on your clothes, be sure your costume blends with your surroundings. Incidentally, smear mud on your face and hands or better yet get a friendly druggist to brew up a face cream that will enable you to tone your face and hands to match your clothing and fit into your environment. The color of your hunting coat and hat may be perfect for the job in hand, but may serve little purpose if your face gleams like the full moon. Definitely, in duck shooting, handsome is as handsome does— as the ducks see you.

Charles Disbrow, a duck hunter of rare ability, painted his gun with rubber cement each year as the duck season approached. This was partly to protect the gun from rust, but more importantly it was to camouflage and dull it. A skillful guide from the Eastern Shore of Maryland kept the working parts of his automatic and the inside of the barrel in perfect shape, but allowed the exterior to rust, claiming "a rusty gun don't shine and sorta blends with the marsh." These two may seem extreme cases, but remember a duck's farsightedness and see how far away you can spot a dark blue gun barrel protruding from a blind. Whether with camouflage or cover, keep your gun concealed until you are ready to shoot.

Next to sharp color contrasts, movement is most likely to disturb ducks. Move as little as possible and when you move, move slowly. Do not stick your head up from blind or boat quickly like a jack-in-the-box, but slowly like the rising sun.

Gun movement is a common fault. Let someone say, "Quiet! Here come three at eleven o'clock," and every man grabs for his gun. This is an entirely natural reaction and the cure lies in advance planning. Have your blind or boat outfitted with racks to hold guns firmly in a *ready* position. I know of no single detail more frequently neglected than this simple but essential matter of a safe, sure, and handy place for the guns. A gun kept in the blind so that it may fall over or which must be hauled into a different position in order to shoot adds a considerable and unnecessary element of danger to duck shooting. Many ducks are spooked, after they start in, by needless gun movement. Last, but by no means least in importance, many *first* shots are missed because the gunner cannot bring his gun quickly and smoothly into position for shooting from some unhandy location.

Whenever you can see other blinds, watch the other fellow and profit by his mistakes. Note how quickly you can see a head raised above the level of the blind, how far you can spot tobacco smoke, and how readily sounds carry across water.

Many of us have to wear glasses in order to see the ducks, but in so doing we certainly make it easier for them to see us. Every care should be exercised by the man with glasses to avoid having them flash danger signals like a heliograph. He should be seated so someone else faces toward the sun when watching for birds. His hat brim should extend to shade his glasses. A doctor friend wears a green-gray sou'wester backward to provide a sort of hood over his spectacles. There may be pleasure but there is little profit to be gained by standing up to scan the horizon with a pair of binoculars. You may see duck, but if you do you can count on the fact they have seen you. I go along with Colonel Sheldon who used to say, "Leave your damn' binoculars home. Leave 'em for the bird watchers. Ducks only visible through binoculars are generally a 'tetch' out of range."

I have one hint about your gear and equipment—a scheme that works for me. I keep a list tacked to the back of the door to the gun cabinet that covers everything from long woolies to licenses and thermos bottles. Every item is stacked on the gunroom floor and checked off on the list before I pack. On earlier trips, before I made a list, I always found I had left something, major or minor, at home.

Lee Smits, famed Detroit newscaster and gunner, writes me on the subject of the essential behavior of the successful duck hunter. I quote his letter in part. "We arrive, of course, at the obvious. Lousy blocks, too few of them, set by an expert whose gun is never under his feet while he eats a sandwich and who shoots to kill will contribute to a much better bag than the best spread in the world with a restless amateur behind it—a guy who just cannot prevent his neck from swiveling while blacks are circling. Hour after hour vigilance, total continuous alertness are the essentials and they pay off best when prospects are dimmest. How many times I have seen dogged alertness pay off! The woods are noisy, or there is a blizzard so the gang hangs out in camp except for some obsessed old coot who sticks to the runway and cheerfully takes the kidding when he comes in at night empty-handed. But from one season to another he is the one who always hangs up his buck, who brings in his limit of duck on a bluebird day when the others quit at noon."

Final Results—
Coykendall's Favorite
Dishes

by Ralf Coykendall, Jr.

Winchester Press and I decided that some readers might feel short-changed if we failed to include the gastronomic delights resultant when my father's advice and suggestions for the proper rigging of decoys are followed. After all, the proof of the pudding is, they say, in the eating; one's waterfowling enjoyment need not end when the sun has set and the last decoy has been picked up. Now comes the "children's hour," when drinks are poured, the day's hits and misses relived, and tales of other days and other shoots are told before the fire. My father was particularly fond of this time of the day and of the dinner that eventually followed any such gathering. I would like to share some of these hours with you.

I think no one will need instruction in the conduct or ingredients of the preprandial ritual, so I will say only that Dad and most of our guests never drank anything other than bourbon and branch water, but a Scotch drinker who had been good company in the blind would not be turned out into the night. Dad kept Scotch in our house as a courtesy. He had no use for gin and other "sissy" liquors, nor did he care for mixed drinks. If you do, you'll be well advised to keep some good bourbon on hand all the same—not only for guests who share the Coykendall preference, but for use in the third (and perhaps best) of the three favorite Coykendall waterfowl recipes which follow.

You will notice that all three are very simple. Indeed, they are artfully simple because simplicity is a true virtue in the preparation of meats so tasty; the last thing you want to do is overpower their flavor with needlessly strong seasonings or sauces.

Before proceeding to the recipes, a few words are in order concerning preparation. Dad believed in hanging "sweet" ducks and breasting "fishy" ones (wood ducks, teal, mallards, and blacks being "sweet;" scaup, whistlers, etc. being "fishy." He had no use for scoters.) "Fishy" ducks were always breasted as soon as possible after shooting, rinsed thoroughly in salted water, and either cooked or frozen. "Sweet" ducks were hung, plucked or breasted, *never rinsed,* and then cooked or frozen. Geese were hung, plucked (preferably by some expert for a fee), and frozen for special occasions.

Christmas Goose

I don't think Dad every really enjoyed eating wild goose until the time when he and I (with the help of our guide) killed six birds one long-ago sundown on Kent Island. It was the guide's wife who gave us the recipe that Dad so much enjoyed and we still use. It's very simple.

Take a plucked goose, stuff it with two bunches of celery (leaves and all) or as much celery as it will hold, and truss the bird; wrap it tightly in heavy-duty aluminum foil and cook in a medium oven for at least four hours. Served with Ev Hoyt's Sauce (made of equal parts of currant jelly, catsup, and dry sherry, melted and stirred slowly together), it makes those hours spent in dank pits all worthwhile.

A Rare Duck

Dad liked good duck served rare, and I mean rare. He would take a properly hung and cleaned greenwing teal (one per person) and after preparing a coarse stuffing of dry bread and apples cut in large pieces, he would stuff the bird, rub it with oil, and roast it in a 450° oven for ten minutes. Served with wild rice and the essential red currant jelly, this either is or isn't one's cup of duck.

Duck Breast A'La Bourbon

Back to the bourbon? Yes, indeed. It is essential here, and this is a recipe for wild duck that will please everyone. It was my father's favorite.

Depending on size of duck(s) and appetite(s), allow the needed number of duck breasts to warm to room temperature.

In a large skillet, slowly melt three tablespoons of red currant jelly and a quarter-pound of butter. After a mixture is fully dissolved, mix in one tablespoon of Worcestershire sauce and one teaspoon each of salt and black pepper.

Turn up the heat under the skillet and add one-third cup of sherry and two-thirds cup of bourbon. Stir. When the mixture comes to a rolling bubble, add the duck breasts and cook, turning occasionally, for five to eight minutes depending on size of duck breasts and degree of rareness desired. Overcooking will toughen the meat.

Serve on wild rice, with more jelly and green peas. I know you will enjoy it. Maybe this should be called "Duck Breasts a'la Coykendall." Good gunning and *bon appétite.*

RCjr

[135]

Grolier also offers merchandise items.
Please write for information.

Sources for Decoys

When this timeless book first appeared in 1955, fine working decoys were readily available from a wide variety of makers for reasonable prices. Unfortunately, all that has changed. The decoys of the 1950s are now expensive antiques and working decoys are themselves fast becoming endangered species. Happily, there are still a handful of people turning out good working decoys in a number of different materials and at affordable prices. Here are a few reliable places:

John Nelson
Route 2
Detroit, TX 75436
Fine hollow-carved pine decoys to special order.

L.L. Bean, Inc.
Freeport, ME 04033
Fine working decoys. Catalog

The Orvis Company
Manchester, VT 05254
First-rate decoys. Catalog

Cabela's
Sidney, NE 69160
Fine working decoys. Catalog